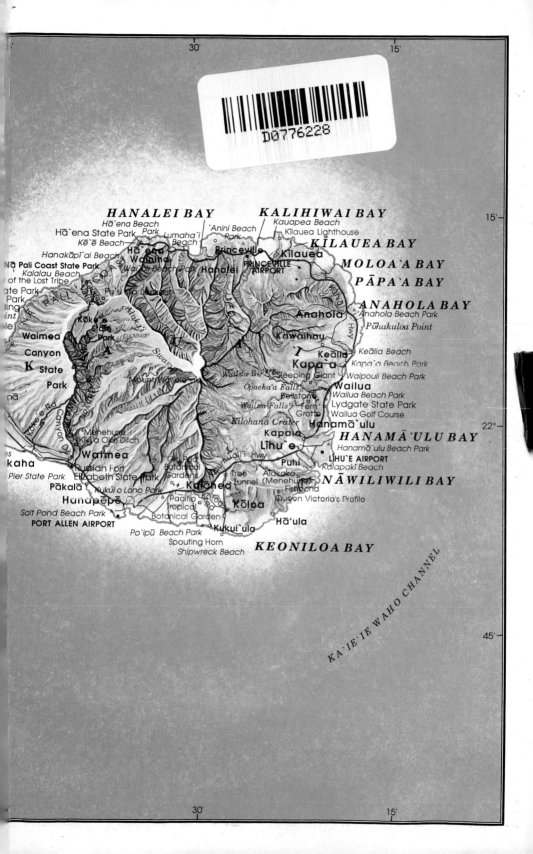

HANALEI BAY

KALIHIWAI BAY

Hā`ena Beach
Park

`Anini Beach
Park

Kauapea Beach

Hā`ena State Park
Kē`ē Beach

Lumaha`i
Beach

Kīlauea Lighthouse

KĪLAUEA BAY

Hanakāpī`ai Beach

Hā`ena
Wainiha

Princeville

Kīlauea

MOLOA`A BAY

Nā Pali Coast State Park
Kalalau Beach
of the Lost Tribe

Wai`oli Beach Park

Hanalei

PRINCEVILLE
AIRPORT

PĀPA`A BAY

ate Park
Park
ing
int
le

Pu`u ka `Ilio Lookout

Waimea
Canyon
K State
Park

Kōke`e
State
Park

A

ANAHOLA BAY

Anahola

Anahola Beach Park
Pōhukuloa Point

Kawaihau

Keālia

Keālia Beach

Mount Wai`ale`ale

Swamp

Kapa`a

Kapa`a Beach Park

Sleeping Giant

Waipouli Beach Park

`Opaeka`a Falls

Wailua Bay

Wailua

Wailua Beach Park

Bellstone

Wailua Falls

Fern
Grotto

Lydgate State Park

Menehune
(Kiki a Ola) Ditch

Kilohana Crater

Wailua Golf Course

Hanamā`ulu

HANAMĀ`ULU BAY

Kōke`e Rd

Kōke`e Rd
Canyon Dr

kaha

Waimea

Kapaia

Līhu`e

Hanamā`ulu Beach Park

Kuamo`o

Kuamo`o Hwy

Russian Fort
Elizabeth State Park

Kuhio Hwy

Puhi

Kuamo`o Hwy

Pier State Park

Pākalā

Kukui o Lono Park

`Ōma`o
Botanical
Gardens

Kalāheo

Tree
Tunnel (Menehune)

LĪHU`E AIRPORT
Kalapakī Beach

Atakoko
(Menehune)
Fishpond

NĀWILIWILI BAY

Hanapēpē

Pacific
Tropical
Botanical Garden

Kōloa

Queen Victoria's Profile

Salt Pond Beach Park

PORT ALLEN AIRPORT

Po`ipū Beach Park

Kukui`ula

Hā`ula

Spouting Horn
Shipwreck Beach

KEONILOA BAY

KA`IE`IE WAHO CHANNEL

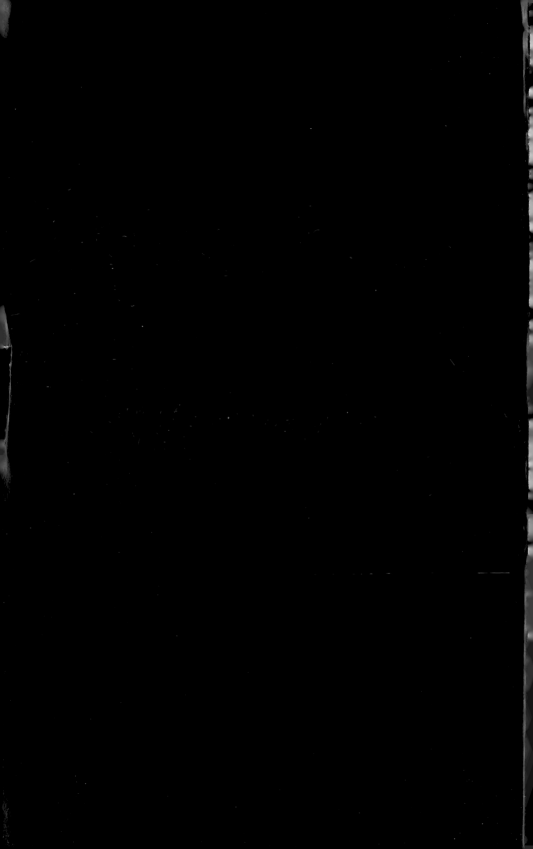

The Essential Guide to Kaua'i

ISLAND HERITAGE
Honolulu, Hawaii

Many people assisted with this project by providing information, and it is impossible to name them all, but we would particularly like to thank the following, who were especially helpful:

Pat Bacon, Bernice Pauahi Bishop Museum; Roselle Bailey; Michaelyn Chou, Hamilton Library, University of Hawai'i; John Clark; Emily Hawkins, Department of Indo-Pacific Languages, University of Hawai'i; Angie Hewitt, *Kaua'i Magazine*; Ruth Horie, Bernice Pauahi Bishop Museum; Wendel Kam, Historic Sites Preservation Office; Koko Kaneali'i; William Kikuchi, Department of Anthropology, Kaua'i Community College; Angela Lee, Bernice Pauahi Bishop Museum; Kelli McCormack, first edition project manager; Pat Palama, Grove Farm Homestead: Joe Recca; Bob Schmitt, State Data Center; Robert Smith; Christine Valles, Office of Hawaiian Affairs; Martha Yent, Historic Sites Preservation Office.

Please address order and
editorial correspondence to:

ISLAND HERITAGE
P U B L I S H I N G
A DIVISION OF THE MADDEN CORPORATION

99-880 IWAENA STREET
HONOLULU, HAWAII · 96701-3202
PHONE 808 · 487 · 7299
FAX 808 · 488 · 2279

THIRD EDITION, THIRD PRINTING -- 1998
Printed in Hong Kong

Produced by:
THE MADDEN CORPORATION

Published by:
ISLAND HERITAGE PUBLISHING
A Division of The Madden Corporation

1995 Editor:
HELEN AVERY DRAKE

Production:
Juanette J. Baysa
J B DESIGNWORKS

Project Coordinator:
SHIU-CHIN LINDA HSU

Photo Editor:
SCOTT RUTHERFORD

Cartography:
ANDREA HINES

Cover Photography by
ANN CECIL

TABLE OF CONTENTS

INTRODUCTION

INTRODUCTION

While Honolulu and Waikīkī are names linked worldwide with images of romance in a tropical Eden, Kaua'i, the northernmost of the main islands in the Hawaiian archipelago, is not a household word. Scenes from Kaua'i are, though, more familiar than most people realize because the island is so popular as a movie location—for stories set in South America, Australia, Africa, Asia and elsewhere, as well as for tropical settings of both the North and South Pacific. Known as 'the Garden Isle', Kaua'i is an out-of-the-way oasis, a haven for those wishing to 'get away from it all'.

KAUA'I IN PARTICULAR

Kaua'i is the oldest of the populated Hawaiian islands and, according to its oral traditions, was the first of the islands to be peopled. Legends say that the Hawaiian gods, from Kahiki (Tahiti), came to Ni'ihau and Kaua'i first, then on through the archipelago.

Kaua'i is also the legendary home of the *Menehune*, a race of tiny people that were exceptional stonemasons and prodigious builders, working only at night and completing each of their projects in a single evening. It is said that if they were struck by sunlight, they turned to stone, and a lot of boulders are billed as petrified *Menehune*.

Other islands also have *Menehune* legends, but on Kaua'i they abound. Most anthropologists believe it likely that people of small stature did inhabit these islands prior to the known Polynesian migrations, and that they have simply shrunk in the telling over many centuries.

Legends of the time before the *Menehune* tell of another people called Mu. This correlates with other prevalent myths of a sunken Pacific continent called Mu (or Lemuria), supposedly predating the more famous Atlantis. Whoever lived on Kaua'i before the Polynesians certainly possessed tools, skills and

knowledge that the Hawaiians did not have, and their exceptional feats of ancient stonework are unique to Kaua'i.

Lying 63 miles north of O'ahu, across the Ka'ie'ie Channel, this 551-square-mile (1427 sq km) island formed by a single volcano is almost round and about 32 miles in diameter, rising to a height of 5243 feet above sea level at Mount Kawaikini near its center. This peak and the adjacent summit of Mount Wai'ale'ale (5148 ft.) catch the moisture-laden prevailing northeast tradewind and are almost constantly shrouded in clouds. Mount Wai'ale'ale is renowned as the wettest spot on Earth. The average annual rainfall is around 40 feet, but precipitation in excess of 50 feet has been recorded in the 900-inch (75-foot) rain gauge (the world's largest) located at the top of the mountain. In contrast, the western (leeward) side of the island gets only around a foot of rain per year.

Most of the mountain rain drains into the Alaka'i Swamp, a high plateau about 10 miles long and covering about 30 square miles. This almost inaccessible area also shelters a number of rare bird and plant species whose natural habitats and ecosystems have been destroyed by large-scale agricultural development and the introduction of new species (80% of Kauaʻi's vegetation is non-native). This natural reservoir feeds the island's extensive system of rivers and streams; Kauaʻi has five major rivers, and the only navigable river in the archipelago.

Another of Kauaʻi's famous and spectacular features is the 25-mile stretch of northern coastline known as Nā Pali (the cliffs). This heavily eroded and thickly forested area is backed by the desert-like red cliffs of Waimea Canyon, on the dry side of the island.

Captain Cook's first landfall in Hawaiʻi was at Waimea, on Kauaʻi's southwest coast, in January 1778. The Hawaiians who watched in awestruck wonder from the shore had never seen large ships and interpreted what they saw as floating islands, the masts leafless trees. These Englishmen, Hawaiʻi's first tourists, spent five days ashore touring the village and environs and, through sign language, learning something of the local culture from their hosts and guides. They traded trinkets for food and the ship's artist, John Webber, drew pictures of the village and its temple *(heiau)*. They left behind the venereal diseases that would quickly decimate the Hawaiian people.

The main center of government was at Wailua, on Kauaʻi's east (windward) coast, and the ruling *aliʻi* was Kaʻeokulani (also known as Kaʻeo). Kaʻeo's son, Kaumualiʻi, was the last ruler of Kauaʻi, and was

Hanalei Bay with familiar 'Bali Hai' in background.

4

never defeated by the conquering Kamehameha, though he pledged his loyalty to Kamehameha in 1810 to avoid bloodshed. His loyalty came into question when, in 1816, he allowed Russian traders to erect a fort, which flew the Russian flag, at the mouth of the Waimea River, but the adventure was short-lived. By agreement with Kamehameha, Kaumuali'i was allowed to retain sovereignty over Kaua'i and Ni'ihau until his death, but when Kamehameha I died, Kamehameha II lured Kaumuali'i to Honolulu where he was imprisoned and forced to marry Kamehameha I's widow, the formidable Ka'ahumanu who, at the same time, also married Kaumuali'i's son. Kaumuali'i died in Honolulu in 1824. Kaua'i's chiefly lines were considered very high, and marital alliances with them—believed to enhance the spouse's *mana* (spiritual power)— were eagerly sought and highly prized. Those who would be Hawai'i's monarchs today, according to the succession named to follow in the event of the death of the Kalākaua line, are of this lineage, being the collateral descendants of King Kalākaua's queen consort, Kapi'olani, directly descended from Kaumuali'i, Kaua'i's last king.

Missionaries and the sugar industry radically changed the face and fortune of Kaua'i. Many missionary descendants became successful planters, and massive irrigation on the island's dry southern plains created vast swards of green. As elsewhere in the islands, agricultural workers from all corners of the world were brought to work in the cane fields. Hawai'i's first sugar plantation was founded in Kōloa in 1835, and, although sugar remains a viable agricultural product, tropical fruits and coffee are becoming increasingly important and lucrative.

Tourism continues to bolster the economy of the island, as with the other Hawaiian islands. This industry had to be completely rebuilt after the devastation left by Hurricane Iniki in 1992. Although, sadly, some Kaua'i businesses incurred massive losses and closed their doors forever, at this writing, a number of Kaua'i's hotels, condominiums, restaurants, rental car companies, shops and other facilities have been rebuilt, refurbished and have reopened. The remarkable resilience of the people of Kaua'i is proof that the *aloha* spirit never dies, and with every challenge grows stronger.

Many of Kaua'i's visitors are regulars, some owning vacation units on the island, and the very rural Hanalei-Hā'ena area provides hideaway homes for some of America's rich and famous as well as less lofty lodgings for an interesting breed of that society's dropouts.

Kaua'i has virtually no manufacturing industry. This lack of development makes Kaua'i the most popular of the islands as a ready-made movie set. The diversity of scenery on such a small island greatly reduces the costs involved in location shooting, and Kaua'i frequently plays the role of locations actually situated many thousands of miles from its shore.

In the 1950s, numerous movies used the Hanalei area as a backdrop, including *Pagan Love Song, Birds of Paradise* and *Miss Sadie Thompson*, but Kaua'i's most famous movie settings of that decade were Lumaha'i Beach and the nearby peak of 'Bali Hai' featured in *South Pacific*.

The '60s brought Elvis Presley to Kaua'i for *Blue Hawaii*, and John Wayne for *Donovan's Reef*. In the '70s, King Kong roamed the Nā Pali Coast; and in the '80s the jungles of Kaua'i

Taro fields saturate Hanalei Valley.

doubled for Vietnam locations in *Uncommon Valor* and *Flight of the Intruder*, and for South America in *Raiders of the Lost Ark*. The Allerton cottage at Kē'ē Beach was the lovers' hideaway in the television movie *The Thornbirds*, set in Australia.

In the '90s, Kaua'i was turned into a place where dinosaurs roam, in Spielberg's mega-movie, *Jurassic Park*.

It was during the final days of filming in 1992 that Hurricane Iniki struck, throwing Spielberg, the cast and crew members into a real-life adventure more frightening than any drama Hollywood could conjure up. In fall of 1994, Kaua'i was transformed into the viruliferous jungles of Africa in *Outbreak*, starring Dustin Hoffman and Morgan Freeman.

NI'IHAU - THE 'FORBIDDEN' ISLE

The privately owned island of Ni'ihau, 17 miles to the west of Kaua'i, was once *kapu* (forbidden) to visitors except by special invitation from the owners. Today, the island is accessible by helicopter via Ni'ihau Helicopter, Inc., which provides one- and two-hour sight-seeing excursions from Kaua'i.

Purchased from Kamehameha V in 1865 by Elizabeth Sinclair of New Zealand for the sum of $10,000, this was established as a cattle ranch for her children. Today, the Robinson family, descendants of her daughter, still owns the island and maintains strict protection of its native heritage, abiding by Mrs. Sinclair's wishes.

Virtually all the island's residents are employed on the Robinson's ranch, or in one of the family's other enterprises on Kaua'i, and seem content in their isolation from the modern world. There is an elemen-

tary school on Ni'ihau where classes are taught in English, according to state law, though on this island Hawaiian is the language of every-day life. Children in higher grades attend school on Kaua'i or on O'ahu at Kamehameha Schools, a respected institution set up for children of Hawaiian ancestry.

Ni'ihau is also known for its small shells which are strung into lovely leis and necklaces and sold at premium prices in stores throughout the islands.

With the development and modernization of much of Hawai'i due to its popularity as a tourist destination, it is important to maintain a connection with its rich cultural history, and the residents of Ni'ihau are to be commended for keeping the integrity of Hawai'i's heritage and language alive for the benefit of future generations.

Beautiful "Secret Beach" on east coast of Kaua'i.

CULTURAL BACKGROUND

Some authorities see in the legends of *Menehune*, particularly prevalent in the oral traditions of Kaua'i, evidence of the presence in these islands of a race of small people who were already resident when the first Polynesians arrived. There is no doubt, though, that voyaging Polynesians did arrive deliberately from the islands of Tahiti and the Marquesas around 400 AD and again around 1100. Some 'experts' claim that the name Hawai'i doesn't actually mean anything in Hawaiian; others see it as an obvious variation of the name of the legendary homeland claimed by all Polynesians: Hawaiki, and the term Hawai'i Nei (literally, Hawai'i here, this Hawai'i) as their way of making a clear distinction in speech between a reference to their present homeland and one to its legendary namesake.

Another interesting theory now rejected by most historians is that the first European to discover these islands was not the famed Captain Cook in 1778, but the Spanish navigator Gaetan, who was blown off course *en route* from the Philippines to Mexico in 1542 and marked these islands on his charts but, finding no gold or silver, never bothered to return. The alleged Spanish visit is dismissed as being, in any case, insignificant and without any lasting effect on the islands' culture, as it was not repeated. This line of reasoning might lead us far from the truth.

Pristine beaches on Kaua'i's north shore.

There are many local legends that allude to white men coming to live amongst the people of these islands in the distant past, and the first English visitors noted distinctly Caucasian features in the faces of some of the natives they encountered. The most apparent evidence in support of this hypothesis is, however, the existence in Hawai'i—but nowhere else in Polynesia—of armor-like, crested, helmet-shaped headgear and ceremonial cloaks in the royal colors of Spain. Some consider this altogether unlikely to be mere coincidence. These magnificent garments were made from many thousands of tiny feathers plucked from small, predominantly black native birds, which were trapped, relieved of their brightly colored feathers and released to produce a new supply—an early example of ecologically efficient management of natural resources.

Be that as it may, Captain Cook did arrive, and with him such sweeping changes that Hawaiian culture was shaken to its very foundations. The first and perhaps most powerful influence to take hold in the islands was the introduction of European diseases to which Hawaiians were not immune, resulting in numerous deaths.

The ambitious young Kamehameha quickly adopted and promoted the technologies of European warfare. Armed with this knowledge, and using his own intelligence and determination, he unseated his cousin Kiwala'o, the hereditary ruler of his home island, Hawai'i, and went on to conquer the rest of the islands.

Trade flourished under Kamehameha's guiding hand, and the islands were swept into the Western world of the nineteenth century, where the old rules no longer applied. For ages the Hawaiian people had been governed by a complex system of *kapu* or restrictions that effectively regulated everything from management of the local ecosystems, through the details of daily life, to the most intimate aspects of spiritual and religious practice. These areas were not demarcated in the world of the Hawaiians. All was one—life was life. Some of the native laws appeared meaningless and merciless to the European mind, and many laws were suspended for immigrant foreigners *(haoles)*, men from visiting ships. The Hawaiian people saw this and worried, wondering why the gods did not intervene.

The loudest death knell for the Hawaiian way of life was rung inadvertently by the powerful Ka'ahumanu, a widow of Kamehameha. At his death, he had named her *kuhina nui* (chief advisor) and set her up as co-regent with his son and heir, Liholiho.

Ka'ahumanu abolished the law prohibiting men and women from dining together, which she found both inconvenient and incompatible with her esteemed position, by persuading Liholiho (Kamehameha II) to sit down and eat with her and his mother, Keopuolani, at a public banquet—an act which produced no response from the gods. She had not realized that the whole *kapu* system would thus come crashing down around the heads of her people, and she had nothing to offer in its place. Their world was shattered—their gods had abandoned them—and the Hawaiians were dazed and spiritually adrift when the first missionaries arrived from New England in 1820.

The Hawaiians had already torn down many of their own temples and chased their priests into hiding. These new invaders met no resistance from the local religion, for there was none.

It was the traders and other white residents of the islands who protested against their moralistic meddling.

As the newcomers acquired more land and as their trading and planting ventures flourished and grew, and as the native population continued to decline, cheap agricultural labor was brought to the islands, first from China, then from Japan, Europe, the Philippines and elsewhere. Thus began the Hawaiian 'melting pot'. As a result of this influx of immigrant workers from a variety of cultural backgrounds, in Hawai'i today, there is no ethnic majority. These people naturally brought with them the languages and customs of their native lands, and with them have enriched the cultural life of Hawai'i.

As a result of the powerful missionary influence, especially over members of the ruling class *(ali'i)*, particularly a few powerful women, Hawaiians signed away their rights and virtually gave their homeland to the newcomers, having never fully grasped the Western concepts of property ownership. Now, with a firmly established toe-hold in Hawai'i's economy, the new rulers, mostly Americans and missionary descendents, eventually wrested political power from the Hawaiian royal line. With the help of representatives of the U.S. government, they set themselves up as the new government of a 'Republic of Hawai'i'. Eventually they persuaded the U.S. Congress to annex them outright, after which they continued to lobby for statehood. None of these sweeping changes had much to do with the actual preferences of the Hawaiian people who were, by this time, a minority.

This exceedingly brief account of Hawaiian history leaves out, of course, details and differing viewpoints of the diverse interest groups involved. Nonetheless, the outcome is the same.

In 1959, Hawai'i was granted U.S. statehood, and is now squarely in the mainstream of modern American life. Its capital, Honolulu, is a thriving business and academic center, the gateway for commerce and cultural exchange with Asia, Australia and the South Pacific.

Throughout the islands, all the modern conveniences of contemporary American life are readily available, yet it is still possible to 'get away from it all'. Hawai'i as a resort destination has something for almost everyone.

Kīlauea area is a wildlife sanctuary for many species of seabirds.

GEOGRAPHY

The Hawaiian archipelago spans 1523 miles (2451 km) and includes 132 islands, reefs and shoals strewn across the Tropic of Cancer, from Kure Atoll in the northwest to underwater seamounts off the coast of the island of Hawai'i in the southeast. All are included in the state of Hawai'i except the Midway Islands, which are administered by the U. S. Navy.

The southernmost territory of the United States lies between latitude 28° 15′ and 18° 54′N and between longitudes 179° 25′ and 154° 40′W, reaching almost as far west as Alaska's Aleutian Islands.

Hawaii's major islands share their tropical latitudes with such urban centers as Mexico City, Havana, Mecca, Calcutta, Hanoi and Hong Kong. The 158th meridian west, which passes through O'ahu's Pearl Harbor, also crosses Point Barrow on Alaska's north coast, Atiu Island in the South Pacific's Cook Islands and Cape Colbeck near the edge of Antarctica's Ross Ice Shelf.

Though the name Hawai'i evokes in the minds of most people images of a tropical paradise in an idealized 'South Pacific', Hawai'i is, in fact, an island group in the North Pacific, uniquely isolated at about 1,000 miles

Kaua'i's etched Nā Pali Coast

from its nearest neighbors - the Line Islands to the south and the Marshall Islands to the southwest. Nothing but open ocean lies between Hawai'i and southern California, 2390 miles (3846 km) to the east-northeast; Japan, 3850 miles (6196 km) to the west-northwest; and Alaska, 2600 miles (4184 km) to the north. The Marquesas, from which at least some of the early Polynesian immigrants came, are 2400 miles (3862 km) to the south-southeast.

Though Hawai'i's land surface adds up to only 6425 square miles (16,642 sq. km), the archipelago, including its territorial waters, covers a total of about 654,500 square miles (1,695,155 sq. km), an area considerably bigger than Alaska and more than twice the size of Texas.

There are eight main islands in the Hawaiian chain, one of which, Kaho'olawe, is not inhabited and, up until 1994, was used by the military for target practice. The tiny island of Ni'ihau is privately owned. Then come the islands of Kaua'i, O'ahu, Moloka'i, Lānai, Maui and Hawai'i (better known as 'the Big Island'). Listed in this order, the islands go from north to south and are arranged by age, with the Big Island being the youngest (and still actively growing).

Sun streams through Waimea Canyon.

CLIMATE AND WEATHER

The climate in Hawai'i is pleasant and equable, that is, it doesn't change much throughout the year—at sea level. The temperature ranges between a daytime high near 90°F (around 30°C) in 'summer' and a nighttime low near 60°F (around 18°C) in 'winter'. There really are no distinct seasons as such. Even in 'winter', the daytime temperature is

INTRODUCTION

Twilight glow over Waimea

usually in the 80s. One's comfort factor depends on what one is used to. People do acclimatize eventually. Those of us who live here start to shiver and bundle up when the mercury plummets to 75 °F (24 °C). The coldest months are February and March; the hottest are August and September.

Despite this lack of strong seasonal variation, Hawai'i is home to an extraordinary diversity of micro-climates, from desert to rain forest. The temperature drops about 3 °F for every thousand feet of increased altitude, a factor which produces seasonal snow on the upper slopes of the Big Island's Mauna Kea.

Rainfall varies dramatically in different parts of each island, from a mere 10 inches annually in some leeward areas to more than 40 feet at the summit of Kaua'i's Mount Wai'ale'ale (the wettest spot on Earth), where it virtually never stops raining. The state's heaviest rains are brought by storms occurring between October and April. A lot of rain is needed to water all this lush tropical foliage, and drought in some areas of the islands is not unheard of.

Fortunately, most of our local rain showers are short. There are, of course, occasions when it rains all day, but these are rare, except in the upper reaches of valleys where the rain clouds never leave for long. The windward areas get far more rain than their leeward counterparts.

There have been only a few damaging storms in Hawai'i, the most devastating one in recent years being in September of 1992 when Hurricane Iniki (strong wind) hit Kaua'i dead on with winds measuring up to 175 m.p.h., and left behind a path of destruction and property loss estimated at more than one billion dollars. With years of clean-up work and extensive rebuilding of roads, homes, hotels, restaurants, and small businesses, a good portion of the island has reestablished itself and returned to normal. Although more than 6,000 Kaua'i residents pulled up stakes and left the island after Hurricane Iniki and many businesses closed for good, the island has undergone a dramatic rebirth, and the community is in many ways more closely bonded than ever before as a result of having struggled through such tough times together.

TIME AND DAYLIGHT

The length of daylight in Hawai'i doesn't vary greatly from one time of the year to the next—only around three or four hours—because of the islands' tropical position. Thus, Hawaiians have never felt any need to save it, and Hawaiian Standard Time is in effect year-round. The time differences between Hawai'i and places that do follow Daylight Savings Time vary by an hour when Daylight Savings is in effect elsewhere. Hawaiian Standard Time is five hours behind New York, four hours behind Chicago, three hours behind Denver and two hours behind San Francisco. It is also eleven hours behind London, nineteen hours behind Tokyo, twenty hours behind Sydney, and twenty-two hours behind Auckland and Suva. Add an hour to all of these when Daylight Savings is in effect elsewhere.

The popular local phrase 'Hawaiian time' simply means 'late'.

THE FLAG

The Hawai'i State flag has served Kingdom, Republic and State and was designed prior to 1816 for King Kamehameha I. Most first-time visitors to Hawai'i are intrigued to note the British Union Jack in the corner. The Union Jack honors Hawai'i's early ties with Britain. The eight horizontal stripes represent the archipelago's eight main islands. Hawai'i's state anthem, 'Hawai'i Pono'ī', is its former national anthem and was composed by King Kalākaua.

Hawai'i's State flag.

LANGUAGE

English became the common language of Hawaiian commerce very early in the era of immigration and economic investment by Americans and other foreigners. And so it remained. The missionaries made sweeping and now irreversible changes in the Hawaiian language when they hurriedly transliterated and transcribed it for print in order to produce bibles. Subsequent efforts to suppress the native tongue were very successful. There are only a few hundred native speakers left, most of whom are either very old or from Ni'ihau. However, a strong grassroots movement to save the language has taken hold in recent years and is gaining widespread support. Virtually everyone in the islands today speaks the American variety of English, with a few local variations on the theme. Some of these should be noted because they are so common.

Perhaps the most important is the local way of giving directions. The cardinal points of the compass on an island are far less relevant than the obvious 'toward the mountain' and 'toward the sea'. A contracted form of the Hawaiian words for these directions is universally used in Hawai'i. Toward the upland (*uka*) is '*mauka*'; toward the sea (*kai*) is '*makai*'. For the other directions, major landmarks are used. The usage is nowhere near as universal on Kaua'i as on O'ahu.

Some people have difficulty with Hawaiian place names and street names. The Hawaiian language is beautiful and only looks intimidating to non-Polynesians because they are not accustomed to seeing so many vowels in a row. Basically, if you just pronounce all the letters individually, you'll be fine. In fact, you might be pronouncing Hawaiian more correctly than a lot of people who are used to it. The glottal stop (written ') is the hard sound created by stopping between vowel sounds, for example, a double 'o' is pronounced like 'oh-oh' in English. In Hawaiian, this is called 'okina. Just stop talking, then start again immediately. The macron (written as ¯ over a vowel), called kahakō in Hawaiian, simply means that vowel is held a little longer—as if it were written twice, which it occasionally is.

Consonants are pronounced the same as in English except that 'w' sounds like 'v' when it immediately precedes a final single vowel and occasionally at other times. Vowels are pronounced as in Spanish or Italian *(ah, eh, ee, oh, oo)*. The vowel combinations—*ai, ae, ao, au, ei, eu, oi* and *ou*—are stressed on the first member and sounded as single units, though the second vowel in the set is truly pronounced and not lost in the combination. Multi-syllabic words are almost always accented or stressed on the next-to-last syllable. No matter how many times you hear the word along the tourist trail, the very special and wonderfully soft Hawaiian word, *aloha*, is NOT correctly pronounced with the accent on the last syllable.

You will often see Hawaiian words written without the *kahakō* and *'okina*. This was the custom of English-speaking people who first transcribed the language, and was common practice until fairly recently. The markings are necessary for correct pronunciation of many words, and for discerning between similarly spelled words with quite different meanings. Government policy is now to insert the correct markings in all Hawaiian words on street and road signs as they are replaced.

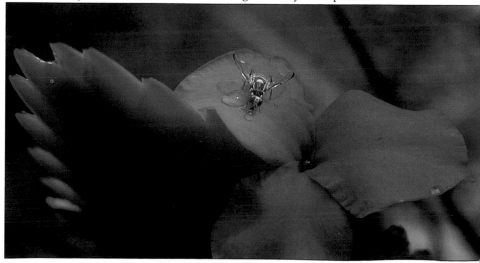

Glory bush and vriesea flowers

The other feature of local language that visitors are bound to encounter is our own brand of 'pidgin' English. It is spiced with words from the rich linguistic heritage brought by people of many lands, but basically, it is English with a bit of Hawaiian, and if you listen carefully, you'll catch on. The idiom and the lilt are peculiar to Hawai'i, but the pronunciation of most words is recognizable.

Lists of commonly used Hawaiian and pidgin English words, along with their meanings and pronunciations, are listed at the Appendix section of this book.

Nā Pali coast sunset.

IN TRANSIT

GETTING HERE

A trip to Kaua'i is especially alluring to travelers seeking a relaxed get-away-from-it-all vacation. The most successful trips are the result of well-organized advance planning, and this section is filled with numerous options for visitors to consider. Because of the vast difference in time and expense, most people choose air travel over sea travel, but the latter is still available; details are discussed below under "Bookings". The time of year to visit the Garden Isle depends on your own schedule and preferences. The largest crowds usually gather in winter and summer months.

CHOOSING LOCATION

The first order of business in planning your stay is to choose your preferred location. Most of Kaua'i's vacation developments are clustered around the island's eastern and southeastern shores, with another concentration in the middle of the northern shore. There are small local communities along the southern shore, and a couple of small military reserves on the western shore. The rest of the island, most of its upland area, is undeveloped, including thousands of acres of forest reserves and state and county parks, where some camping is permitted.

SELECTING LODGING

Kaua'i has both glamorous suites and idyllic rural retreats, with choices ranging from luxurious to rustic, with lots of offerings in between. While the island boasts several excellent hotels, most of its resort accommodations are condo-miniums. Many visitors, especially those accompanied by children, prefer these self-contained apartment facilities. This option can be less expensive and may offer travelers more privacy and independence.

Hotels are the favorite of those

Po'ipū Beach at sunset

who wish to be pampered during their stay. Most of our hotels are staffed by courteous, friendly, and efficient people, and offer guests a wide selection of activities. Private vacation homes are also plentiful and ideal for those on longer visits or with large families. Bed-and-breakfast (B&B) guestrooms and cottages are available throughout the island for those who prefer a more intimate atmosphere. For nature lovers and the budget-minded, rustic cabins and campsites are available, but should be reserved way in advance, as they are in limited supply. For a comprehensive listing of the various types of lodging as well as local reservation services, refer to the ACCOMMODATION section of this book.

WHAT TO BRING

The usual attire on Kaua'i is casual, and apparel known elsewhere as 'summer clothing' is worn year-round in this land of perpetual spring and summer. Shorts are acceptable almost anywhere, though most businesses require customers to wear shoes (rubber thongs will usually suffice). Comfortable walking shoes are a must. Sleeveless or short-sleeved shirts are usually best for day wear, but long sleeves, or even a jacket or sweater, may be needed for cool winter evenings and air-conditioned buildings. Deluxe restaurants sometimes have a dress code requiring men to wear jackets, but not usually ties.

PERMITS AND LICENSES

Licenses or permits are required for some activities in which visitors may choose to participate. The most common is driving. Any visitor who drives in Hawai'i must have a valid license from another state or Canadian province or a current international driver's license issued in another country.

Camping permits are required for

Menehune Fishpond was credited to the legendary race of small people.

public parks that allow camping. All hunting requires a license, as does fresh-water fishing; none is required for recreational ocean fishing. Details for sporting licenses are discussed in the SPORTS section.

Those wishing to indulge in the romance of tropical nuptials need a license, which may be obtained from the State Department of Health in Honolulu or from one of many marriage license agents licensed by the Kaua'i County Board of Health (P.O. Box 671, Lihu'e, Hawai'i 96766;

808-245-4495 M-F, 8 a.m.-4 p.m.) Licenses are issued immediately after application, usually within twenty minutes, and expire after 30 days. They are only valid in Hawai'i, and the nominal fee is payable in cash at the time of filing.

Numerous local companies specialize in wedding services, some of which are described under "Island Weddings" in the ET CETERA section of this book; others are can be found under "Wedding" in the Kaua'i Yellow Pages.

BOOKINGS

To book your air or cruise tickets, lodging, and any tours you may wish to arrange in advance, we recommend using a travel agent. You could spend days chasing specifics and comparing prices, but travel agents have the information at their fingertips and they know their sources well. It costs you no more, as the agents' commission is paid by the provider, not the customer. In many cases, the agent can offer you a better deal than you could get if you booked directly. Many airlines and hotels also give priority bookings made through agents, as they are

generally less likely to be canceled.

If you plan to stay in a bed-and-breakfast accommodation or lease a private vacation home, there are several local reservation services available to assist you. Many of these services charge a nominal booking fee, however, it can turn out to be a savings for you in the long run, reducing time, energy and money otherwise spent on long distance calls and researching on your own. For a listing of such services, refer to the ACCOMMODATION section of this book.

Airlines

Our island state is such a popular destination that, though it is accessible only by air or sea, airfares are kept low through volume and competition. There are many airlines serving the Hawaiian Islands, most landing at Honolulu International Airport. Flight times are roughly five hours from California, nine hours from Chicago, eleven hours from New York, eight hours from Tokyo and nine and a half hours

from Sydney. Domestic carriers providing service to and from the U. S. mainland are: **American Airlines, Continental, Delta, Hawaiian Airlines, Northwest Airlines, TWA and United Airlines.** United Airlines offers flights from San Francisco and Los Angeles directly to Kahului, Maui, and from San Francisco to Kailua-Kona on the Big Island of Hawaii. Carriers providing service between the

Hawaiian Islands are **Aloha Airlines, Aloha Island Air, Hawaiian Airlines, Mahalo,** and **American Airlines**.

Foreign carriers currently serving Honolulu are **Air New Zealand, Canadian Airlines, China Airlines,** **Garuda Indonesia, Japan Air Lines, Korean Air, Philippine Airlines, Qantas** and **Singapore Airlines,** among others. Consult your travel agent for the latest details and flight schedules.

Cruise Lines

Traveling to Hawaii by cruise ship is not easy these days, least of all to Kaua'i. Most of the cruise lines that make stops at our islands--**Cunard, American,** and **Royal Viking**--are of foreign registry and are forbidden by

Harvesting taro, a Hawaiian staple, in Hanalei.

U. S. law from transporting American citizens from one U. S. port to another U. S. port. This law, the Jones Act, was passed in 1896. Thus, if you board a foreign vessel in New York or California, you may visit Hawai'i, but cannot make it or any other U. S. port your final destination. You may, if you board a ship in another country, make Hawai'i or another American port your final destination, but most cruise operators today do not encourage one-way traffic. Still, it is possible, and there is no more beautiful way to arrive here than by sea.

American Hawaii Cruises has two ships, the *SS Constitution* and the *SS Independence,* that cruise the Hawaiian waters departing Honolulu on a weekly basis and docking in Kaua'i, Maui and the Big Island. The ships provide visitors with first class service and exquisite panoramic vistas by sea, as well as a selection of land tours at each island stop-over. Reservations can be made by calling (800) 765-7000.

Sight-seeing Tours

Your travel agent can book tours for you in advance, or you may wish to contact one of the following activity planners on Kauai.

Many visitors prefer to book tours after arrival and a bit of scouting around.

Activity Information Center	(808) 245-3300
Captain's Cargo Company	(808) 338-0333
Hawaiian Fantasy Adventures	(808) 246-0111
Hawaiian Style Tours & Activities	(808) 822-6960
KVRA Activities	(808) 822-7755
Ray's Rentals & Activities	(808) 822-5700
The Fun Lady	(808) 822-7759

HONOLULU INTERNATIONAL AIRPORT

This is one of the busiest airports in the world, serving as gateway between East and West. Passengers arriving from the U.S. mainland or from other countries emerge from this vast complex on the ground level of the main terminal building. The airport's second level services mainland and overseas departures.

Most arriving and departing interisland flights service passengers from the recently completed interisland terminal, located next to the main terminal at the westward end of the airport. This new building is much larger than the former interisland terminal, with expanded shops, eating facilities and waiting areas, which allow for more convenient and comfortable interisland travel than was previously available.

KAUA'I AIRPORTS

Lihu'e has a lovely airport, with all the usual amenities such as book and souvenir shops, bar, snack shop and visitor information desks. There are no customs and immigration facilities, as passengers arriving from other countries must be cleared in Honolulu before continuing their journey to Kaua'i. Six car rental agencies are conveniently located directly across from the arrival portals of the airport. Shuttle buses to rental cars pick up customers in this area; taxis are situated at the front of the terminal. Arrangements for transportation by shuttle buses or vans for guests of the major hotels may be made in advance.

Princeville Airport is a small airport located on the north shore and utilized by private planes, one commercial airline **(Aloha Island Air)**, and a helicopter company **(Papillon Hawaiian Helicopters).** The terminal has a cafe lounge and free parking, as well as two rental car companies (**Hertz** and **Avis**). The adjacent headquarters of Papillon Hawaiian Helicopters has a gift shop.

Special Lei Greetings

One of the loveliest Hawaiian customs involves the giving of a garland of island flowers as a gesture of *aloha* on special occasions. To experience this upon your arrival at Lihu'e Airport, contact a local greeting service in advance. Two companies serving Kaua'i you may want to call are **Greeters of Hawaii** (808-245-1679; fax: 245-4553) or **Trans Hawaiian Kaua'i** (808-245-5108). If you prefer being "lei'd" upon your arrival at the Honolulu Airport, you can contact **All Island Greeters** (808-836-5631), **Kenui Aloha** (808-523-2825) or **Leis of Hawaii** (808-732-7385) in Honolulu.

Transportation

Lihu'e Airport is about two miles from town, nineteen miles from Po'ipū, twelve miles from Kapa'a and thirty-five miles from Hanalei.

Princeville Airport is about two miles from Princeville, three miles from Hanalei and six miles from Hā'ena.

An overcast afternoon at Brennecke's

Transportation

BUS

Kaua'i now has a bus system, put into service in 1992 after Hurricane Iniki. Originally called the "Iniki Express", it has been renamed simply the "Kaua'i Bus". Initially, the federal government subsidized its operation as part of its disaster relief effort and it was free of charge. Since 1995, passengers are charged a nominal fare to ride. The bus travels all around the island (area includes Kekaha to Hanalei) and is an economical service for visitors and residents alike.

Currently, the bus runs hourly, so plan your trip and leave plenty of time if you need to transfer to the Lihue Extension. Be aware that there is no evening or Sunday bus service available. You can pick up a bus schedule free at Lihu'e Airport Information Desk, or by sending a self-addressed stamped envelope to County of Kaua'i Transportation Agency, 4280-A Rice Street, Lihu'e, Hawai'i 96766. For further information call 241-6410.

TAXI

Taxicab companies providing service to and from Lihu'e Airport include **ABC Taxi of Kaua'i** (808-822-7641), **Hanamaulu Taxi** (808-245-3727) and **Kaua'i Cab Service** (808-246-9554). The standard metered cost of a journey is $2.00 per mile, plus $2.00 at the meter drop, so

this can be an expensive way to travel if you have far to go. There is normally an extra charge for each piece of luggage. **North Shore Cab & Tours** (808-826-6189) services Princeville Airport, and runs about $12 between the airport and Hanalei.

RENTAL CAR

At Lihu'e Airport, six rental car agencies have service desks facing the baggage claim areas opposite the main terminal building, with offices near the airport. Cars are returned by customers at nearby lots (follow the signs) on the airport premises, then shuttle buses ferry passengers back to the terminal to catch outbound flights. For additional information, see GETTING AROUND.

At Princeville Airport, rental cars are available only through Avis and Hertz, both of which have offices and vehicles on premises.

Some hotels offer combination room and rental car packages, and some airlines offer fly/drive packages for less than you would pay if booked separately. Inquire at your travel agency for details.

LIMOUSINE

Special arrangements may be made in advance to be met at the airport by a limousine service. The following companies offer service to all parts of the island: **Custom Limo** (808-246-6318), whose vehicles hold up to six passengers, and **North**

Shore Limousine (808-826-6189), offering two sizes of limousines accommodating up to six or eight passengers. Hourly rates start at about $74.00 net per hour, with a two-hour minimum. Amenity charges, 4% state tax and tip are additional.

24

Nā Pali coast is one of Kauaʻi's major attractions.

GETTING AROUND

A single main highway runs near the coastline and around most of Kaua'i, cutting inland across the southeastern tip of the island and stopping altogether at Polihale on the west coast and Hā'ena on the north coast. The southern portion is called Kaumuali'i and the western and northern section, Kūhiō. Between these ends of the road is the dramatic 25-mile stretch of Nā Pali coastline. The options for getting around are via the public Kaua'i Bus, rental car or the most costly method, taxi. Tours are available on land, by sea or in the air, and bicycling and hiking are very popular on this island.

TOURS AND RENTALS

Guided tours are numerous and varied. There are dozens of companies listed under "Tours" in the Kaua'i Yellow Pages. Exploring on your own in a rented vehicle is the other option.

Air Tours

Scenic flights over Kaua'i are almost indispensable. Much of the island's spectacular natural scenery is otherwise inaccessible except by arduous and sometimes dangerous hiking and mountain climbing, but some of it is not risky or strenuous at all. Although the bird's-eye view has its own risks, it provides a magnificent vantage point for taking in Kaua'i's remarkable natural beauty. Do this first, and the rest of your sight-seeing on Kaua'i will be greatly enriched.

Fixed-wing overflights are available only from other islands as part of multi-island packages. On Kaua'i, helicopters are ideal for getting into the nooks and crannies of this rugged terrain. So popular has this sight-seeing sensation become that there are some twenty helicopter tour companies operating on Kaua'i and many residents jokingly tell visitors that Kaua'i's island bird is the "whirlybird".

The largest helicopter company is Princeville's **Papillon Hawaiian Helicopters** (808-826-6591; 800-367-7095), operating with six choppers on Kaua'i (with operations on each island) and able to accommodate large groups. Their unique wilderness landings and drop-offs allow passengers an isolated natural experience of the island. **Jack Harter Helicopters** (808-245-3774) operates out of Līhu'e and is considered one of the best. All flights are piloted by Harter himself, who has been flying helicopters for more than thirty years. His flights take an hour and a half and are enriched by his deep love for and thorough knowledge of the island. Three flights are available Monday through Friday, weather permitting. These tours are booked well ahead, so it is advisable to make advance reservations. To those would-be customers who cannot be accommodated, Harter's staff recommends **Will Squyres Helicopter Service** (808-245-7541), offering six hour-long flights daily. Squyres has been piloting helicopters for almost as long as Harter and his tours reveal a broad knowledge of Kaua'i.

If neither of these is available at a

time to fit your schedule, choose a company where the owner is the pilot and has an air taxi license (not all have this, and getting it requires more rigorous testing than a simple operator's license). Also, choose a flight that spends at least an hour in the air; anything quicker will have the scenery whizzing past so fast you'll hardly glimpse a feature of the landscape before it's gone.

Safari Helicopters (808-246-0136; 800-326-3356), is run by Preston Myers, a pilot with over 30 years in the industry. Operating out of Līhu'e Heliport, it offers several tours ranging from 35 to 65 minutes

in length. Myers was the first in the state to fly what he calls the "Cadillac of sight-seeing helicopters", the ASTAR 350. The choppers are air-conditioned, seat up to six passengers and allow unobstructed panoramic views of 180 degrees.

Air Kaua'i Helicopter Tours (808-246-4666; 800-246-7666), **South Sea Tours & Helicopters** (808-245-2222; 800-367-2914) and **Ohana Helicopter Tours** (owned and operated by Hawaiian born pilot Bogart Kealoha, 808-245-3996; 800-222-6989) operate out of Līhu'e Airport. Inquire about shuttles to and from hotels.

Water Tours

The next most exciting and not-to-be-missed excursion on Kaua'i is a boat trip down the Nā Pali Coast. It doesn't matter if you've seen the coast from the air; this gives you an entirely different perspective -- the

functional equivalent of rafting down the Colorado River after flying around in the Grand Canyon. Kaua'i's monolithic pinnacles look particularly awesome from the bottom. This trip runs during calm surf conditions in

Zodiacs brave rough winter waters on the Nā Pali Coast.

the summer months, May through September, and occasionally in winter-time when the ocean allows it. Water tours of the southern shores are available year-round, and there is whale watching in this region as well.

Short Excursions

There are four basic types of boat trips: by small power cruiser, by power-driven inflatable boat (usually called Zodiac, a brand name), by sailboat and by kayak.

At least one company, **Hanalei Sea Tours** (808-826-7254), offers both power catamaran and Zodiac options. The most popular of these options is the Zodiac. The most experienced company is **Captain Zodiac Raft Expeditions**, hosting tours of the Nā Pali coast since 1974. Another operator is **Nā Pali Adventures**, which operates power catamarans.

Not all the tour guides and pilots are equally experienced, however (this is a job popular with California youth), and the bits of Hawaiian 'history' related by some of them are quite creative and original. If you have a choice, go with a guide who is native to the island, or at least a longtime resident of Hawai'i.

Captain Zodiac Raft Expeditions (800-422-7824; 808-826-9371) has special status as the only Zodiac operator with permission from the state to land on the Nā Pali Coast. Their most popular Nā Pali trip is their five-hour excursion, cruising through sea caves and under waterfalls (when ocean conditions permit), and stopping for lunch, snorkeling and onshore exploration at Nu'alolo Kai, a beach that is inaccessible except by sea. Shorter trips ranging from two to four hours in length are also offered. Prices range from $65 per person (3-hr. afternoon excursion) to $105 per person (5-hr. day expedition), depending on the particular trip chosen, with reduced rates for children age 12 and under. (Note: please confirm current prices when you call.) They also offer a drop-off/ pick-up service (May 15 - Sept. 15) for campers and hikers who wish to explore Kalalau and Miloli'i State Park. Tour captains share their knowledge on the various animals and sea creatures which may be spotted along the way, and relate to passengers the history and legends of the area. This company assisted in the formation of the Hawaii Whale Research Foundation, and aided the Cousteau Society with its research in 1988.

Zodiacs, however, are not for everyone. They are fun, but the ride can be rough, is almost assuredly wet, and there are no restrooms on board. They are definitely to be avoided by pregnant women, or individuals with a history of back or neck problems. Powered catamaran is a good alternative for those who prefer a fast but smoother ride. **Nā Pali Adventures** in Hanalei (808-826-6804; 800-659-6804) is one of the many tour companies that offers good quality rides. For those preferring a drier, even smoother ride, cabin cruisers are the answer. One of the most popular is **Lady Ann Cruises,** which leaves from Hanalei, and can be booked through **Hawaii Rafting Expeditions** in Waimea (808-335-9909).

Most north shore tour companies also offer south shore snorkeling and whale-watching expeditions during the winter months when the surf pounds the north shore with twenty- to thirty-foot waves. In addition, **Capt. Andy's Sailing Adventures** (808-822-7833) offers sailing/ snorkeling excursions, sunset sails and seasonal whale watching along the south coast aboard a 55-foot catamaran, "Spirit of Kauai".

For a delightfully different experience, try Island Adventure's Kaua'i River Adventure (808-245- 9662), which goes up the Hule'ia River, passing the famous Alakoko (Menehune) Fishpond, and visiting the upstream filming sites of the movies Raiders of the Lost Ark (where Indiana Jones swung from the vines of a "South American" jungle) and Uncommon Valor (where Gene Hackman thrashed his way through the tropical forest of "Vietnam"). Each person paddles his/her own individual 'royak', a

cross between a kayak and a canoe, passing through the scenic Hule'ia National Wildlife Refuge. The vessels are extremely stable in the water and life jackets are provided, making the four-hour trip safe for non-swimmers as well as children.

On the east coast, a relaxed, tranquil cruise up the broad, winding Wailua River is one of Kaua'i's most popular visitor activities. These tours, run by Smith's Motor Boat Service (808-822-5213) and Wai'ale'ale Boat Tours (808-822-4908) visit the famous Fern Grotto, with narration on the upstream leg and Hawaiian entertain- ment on the return. Smith's, the granddaddy of Wailua riverboat cruises (since 1947), also offers a twilight trip, a visit to the Fern Grotto by torchlight and candlelight and a floating lu'au. For do-it-yourself excursions and boat rentals, refer to the SPORTS & RECREATION section.

Tranquil Wailua river offers many water and boating activities.

Extended Cruises

American Hawaii Cruises (800-765-7000) operates seven-day cruises around the Hawaiian Island chain, stopping at Kaua'i's Nāwiliwili Harbor. They run two historic, 30,000-ton sister ships, the *SS Constitution* and the *SS Independence*, built in 1951. The *Constitution* was re-christened in 1982 by Her Royal Highness Princess Grace of Monaco, who sailed aboard the ship in 1956 with her wedding party. The two ships were refurbished in 1980 and have been serving Hawai'i ever since. More recent refurbishment of the two ships was done in 1994 and 1995. Starting from Honolulu, the vessels make similar rounds, visiting the islands of Hawai'i, Kaua'i and Maui, with ports of call at Hilo, Kona, Nāwiliwili and Kahului, where they cross paths. Shipboard accommodations (cabins, staterooms and suites) range in size, location and price and determine the overall cruise fare. Besides an abundance of food, entertainment and recreational facilities, the optional planned activities on board and shore excursions will keep energetic passengers bustling.

Land Tours

There are only a few options for getting around on land. Buses come in several varieties; numerous types of private vehicles can be rented; there are horseback and bicycle tour companies; and, of course, there are lots of places to go on foot.

GUIDED GROUP BUS AND VAN TOURS

Huge buses that hold fifty or more passengers are good for keeping large tour groups together, and they are air-conditioned. Several smaller buses are also used by tour companies and these, though not always air-conditioned, afford a more intimate atmosphere for the passengers. Best of all are the increasingly popular mini-buses or large vans that are used by many local tour companies. These allow the most personalized service of all. **Trans Hawaiian Kaua'i** (808-245-5108) offers many different routes to the most popular destinations.

North Shore Cab & Tours not only runs a taxi service, but also offers a comprehensive five-hour tour out of the Hanalei area called the "Best of Kaua'i", which visits the north and east shores, includes a boat ride to Fern Grotto, and ends with a helicopter tour out of Princeville Airport. Tours are conducted in 15-passenger air-conditioned vans, and can be arranged (for a minimum booking of twelve) by calling (808-826-6189). Shorter tours are also available from North Shore Cab. **Gray Line-Kaua'i** (808-245-3344), **Kaua'i Island Tours** (808-245-4777) and **Akita Enterprises** (808-245-5344) can accommodate those interested in general sight-seeing routes on buses of various sizes and vans.

Most tour operators offer reduced prices for children. Advance reservations should be made for all tours; most hotels have courtesy desks in their lobbies where these can be easily and quickly arranged. Also, many of the bed-and-breakfast hosts can be valuable resources for tour tips, and many offer to assist guests with reservations.

FOUR-WHEEL DRIVE

A unique tour experience is that offered by **Kauai Mountain Tours** (808-245-7224), the only operator licensed to go into Kōke'e State Park. They travel roads that wind through the forest and down the back of Waimea Canyon, occasionally fording streams along the way, and the well-informed narrative enhances appreciation of the surrounding environment. A picnic lunch prepared by the Green Garden Restaurant of Hanapēpē is another highlight of this all-day tour.

Warm winds, calm waters, and exquisite isolation.

LIMOUSINE

If you prefer a more pampered excursion, there are limousines at your service at hourly rates. **North Shore Limousine** (808-826-6189) and **Custom Limo** (808-246-6318) offer private tours, as does **Kaua'i Island Tours** (808-245-4777), and all can arrange for a gourmet picnic and other special touches upon request.

MOPED

You can motor along on two wheels for a more casual, outdoor touring experience. Renters of mopeds must be licensed and over the age of eighteen. Those not holding major credit cards must leave substantial cash deposits.

Pedal & Paddle in Hanalei (808-826-9069) and Kapa'a (808-822-2005), and **Honda Two Wheels** in Kapa'a (808-822-7283) rent these low-powered, slow-moving scooters. Drivers of mopeds should be especially aware of other vehicles and move to the side of the road allowing cars and trucks to pass.

CAR RENTAL

Kaua'i has seven car rental agencies, most of which provide current standard American and Japanese sedans and compacts, and some have convertibles, station wagons and even vans. **Alamo, Avis, Budget, Dollar, Hertz** and **National** have facilities at Lihu'e Airport. **Avis** and **Hertz** also service Princeville Airport. A local company, **Westside U-Drive,** serves the Po'ipū area exclusively, offering free delivery and pick-up of your car at your hotel or condo.

BICYCLE

On Kaua'i, traffic is generally light, especially in early morning, and poses little hazard to alert cyclists. Pedaling along under your own steam provides an even closer experience of the natural beauty of Kaua'i's tropical environment. Although most of the roads are good, shoulders are narrow to nonexistent, so taking extra caution and wearing protective gear is recommended .

Three companies provide escorted bicycle tours. **Kayak Kaua'i Outfitters** in Kapa'a (822-0577) has combination bike/snorkel tours offered daily. **Outfitters Kaua'i** in Po'ipū (742-9667) leads mountain bike excursions through Kōke'e State Park's backroads. **Kaua'i Downhill** (245-1774) offers a downhill bicycle tour from Waimea Canyon (see SPORTS).

Touring bicycles can be rented from **Kayak Kaua'i Outfitters** (822-0577) in Kapa'a, **Outfitters Kaua'i** in Po'ipū (742-9667) and **Pedal & Paddle** in Hanalei (826-9069) and Kapa'a (822-2005). If you need emergency repairs, **Bicycle John** in Kapa'a (822-3495) or Lihu'e (245-7579) and **Bicycles Kaua'i** in Kapa'a (822-3315) offer service in a half-day to a day, depending on the problem.

EXPLORING

Sight-seeing
Historic sites
Parks and gardens
Beaches

SIGHT-SEEING

K aua'i has a splendid array of sights worthy of visitor attention. Descriptions follow a counterclockwise sequence around the island. Be on
the lookout along the roads for the Hawai'i Visitors Bureau 'Hawaiian
warrior' signs that indicate points of interest and other places.

SCENIC AREAS

There are few places in Hawai'i
that are not scenic—especially on
Kaua'i—so we here draw attention to
some of the more spectacular natural
features. Details of historic sites and
buildings, museums, sacred sites,
parks and gardens are included
under specific sub-headings in this
section.

The most famous area of this
beautiful island is its spectacular **Nā
Pali Coast,** an awesome array of
perpendicular cliffs and eroded
pinnacles punctuated by waterfalls
and hanging valleys that end
abruptly in sheer palisades at the

sea. The best known of these valleys
is **Kalalau,** which can be reached via
an eleven-mile, cliff-hugging trail that
traverses several smaller valleys
along the way.

Above Kalalau are a couple of
spectacular viewpoints, **Kalalau
Lookout** and **Pu'u o Kila Lookout,**
reached by road from the other side
of the island, that afford breathtaking
vistas. Alternatively, they offer the
fascinating experience of watching a
cloud coming, being surrounded by
it, and watching it pass on, sometimes filling the valley entirely, then,
as it disperses, dramatically unveiling

34

Some of the island's best hiking is found on the Nā Pali Coast.

the scene four thousand feet below.

The lookouts and the surrounding forest preserve are located in **Kōke'e State Park,** adjacent to the **Alaka'i Wilderness Preserve,** and the thirty-square-mile **Alaka'i Swamp,** the natural drainage sump for Mount Wai'ale'ale and the source of most of the island's rivers and streams.

The second most famous natural feature on Kaua'i is the colossal **Waimea Canyon,** touted by tourist literature as the 'Grand Canyon of the Pacific'. Some credit Mark Twain with this analogy; others claim he never set foot on this island. In any case, the canyon, twelve miles long and three thousand feet deep, is spectacularly beautiful and, though hardly comparable to that great chasm of the American Southwest, is still high on the list of the world's magnificent sights. It is especially awesome when considered in relation to the size of the island.

Near its mouth, just above the town of Waimea on the island's southern shore, are the remains of **Kīkī a Ola** or the **Menehune Ditch,** an irrigation canal and a prodigious feat of ancient engineering. The remaining ruins are located, not at all conspicuously, at the end of Menehune Road, in Waimea off Kaumuali'i Highway.

At the far end of the road on the western shore is **Polihale State Park,** a long strip of sandy beach tucked at the base of sheer gray cliffs, with Ni'ihau and its offshore islet, Lehua, visible across the Kaulakahi Channel. The park contains the ruins of two *heiau* and a sacred spring. The last five miles of the access road is unpaved and can become boggy in wet weather.

Though there were a few villages along the coast in ancient times, the nearest town is now Kekaha. Here, Mānā Road (550) turns off Kaumuali'i Highway (50) then becomes Kōke'e Road and climbs twenty miles to

Hanalei Bay is subject to strong currents during winter months.

Kōke'e Lodge and Kōke'e State Park. Also number 550 is Waimea Canyon Drive, which starts at Kaumuali'i Highway in Waimea and meets Kōke'e Road about halfway up the mountain. It is strongly recommended that you take one route up and the other down, as the views from each are magnificent and quite different.

It was at Waimea that Captain Cook first made landfall in the Hawaiian Islands, in January 1778, and there is a monument to him in the middle of town. On the eastern bank at the mouth of the Waimea River stand the ruins of **Fort Elizabeth**, built by the Russians in 1816.

warrior marks a scenic overlook into the **Hanapēpē Valley.** This is a vista worth stopping for. Just west of Kalāheo, you will find the turnoffs leading to **Kukui o Lono** (*makai* of the highway on Pāpālima Road), the former estate of Walter McBryde, encompassing a Japanese garden and a 9-hole golf course, and **'Olu Pua Botanical Gardens** (*mauka*, directly off the highway), a former plantation manager's estate and gardens.

Not far east of Kalāheo, a turn *makai* onto Kōloa Road (530) will take you, after a short distance, to Hailima Road (an inconspicuous fork) and the Visitor Center of the **National Tropical Botanical Garden,** a tropical

Kīkī a Ola, the Menehune Ditch

Near Hanapēpē, between the Port Allen Airport and Salt Pond Beach Park are the ancient **Salt Ponds.** There are no signs to lead you there. Turn *makai* off Kaumuali'i Highway (50) just west of Hanapēpē town at the sign pointing toward the Veterans Cemetery; drive past the cemetery then west on Lokokai Road until you can see them. East of Hanapēpē, a Hawai'i Visitors Bureau

plant research facility. Farther down Kōloa Road, you will arrive at Old Kōloa Town, where another turn *makai* will take you past Kūhiō Park to the Spouting Horn. There are holes in this coastal shelf where the force of waves under the rock causes water to spurt into the air, but one waterspout shoots far higher than the others. On a mildly windy day with a small ocean swell, it has been seen to go as high as thirty to forty feet.

Taking Maluhia Road (520) north from Old Kōloa Town, you will drive through Kaua'i's famous **Tunnel of Trees,** rows of huge eucalyptus. Prior to 1992's Hurricane Iniki, the tree branches met overhead in a continuous leafy canopy, and, although the trees are still a lovely and stately landmark, they are now a few years away from regenerating to form a completed archway. Along Kaumuali'i Highway (50) just west of Puhi, there is a warrior marker indicating **Queen Victoria's Profile,** which some say can be discerned in the outline of the Hā'upu Range (now often called the Hoary Head Range) to the south.

At the eastern edge of Kukui Grove Center, just west of Līhu'e, a turn *makai* onto Nāwiliwili Road (58) will take you to **Nāwiliwili Harbor.** Only about a hundred yards *mauka* of the terminus of this road, on the eastern side, is the entrance to the **Menehune Gardens.** Nāwiliwili Harbor and Kalapakī Beach can also be reached by following Rice Street through Līhu'e. Going west at Nāwiliwili Harbor on Wa'apa Road, you will see the Hawai'i Visitors Bureau marker for the **Menehune Fishpond;** turn *mauka* onto Hulemalu Road. At the top of the hill is a scenic lookout over this ancient aquacultural

37

Waimea Canyon—an anomaly in the Hawaiian Islands

structure, known to Hawaiians as Alakoko.

Following the same road past the harbor and straight into Līhu'e, on Rice Street, you will pass the **Kaua'i Museum**. Only a little farther along the same route is the junction of Kaumuali'i (50) and Kūhiō (56) Highways. Straight ahead on Kaumuali'i and just past the underpass, a Hawaiian warrior marker indicates the Ho'omana Road turnoff to the **oldest Lutheran Church** in the state, built in 1883.

A turn at Līhu'e junction onto Kūhiō Highway leads to Kapaia where Mā'alo Road (583) turns *mauka* and leads to a scenic overlook of **Wailua Falls**. Kūhiō Highway continues through Hanamā'ulu to **Wailua,** the home base of Kaua'i's ruling chiefs prior to European settlement of the island. Stone remnants of ancient buildings abound in the area. On the coast between Wailua Golf Course and the Wailua River Bridge, is **Lydgate State Park,** where the ruins of Hauola Pu'uhonua and Hikina a Kalā Heiau stand in a coconut grove. Along the southern bank of the river, *mauka* of the bridge, are Wailua Marina and **Smith's Tropical Paradise,** a botanical garden.

Across the bridge and just *mauka* of Kūhiō Highway on Kuamo'o Road (580) is the Coco Palms Resort (currently closed for renovation), and a little farther along the road on the opposite side are **Holoholokū Heiau** and **Pōhaku-ho'ohānau** (Royal Birthing Stones). A little farther up the hill, just before the 'Ōpaeka'a Falls/Wailua River lookout, a dirt road on the left (opposite a public comfort station) leads to the ruins of **Poli'ahu Heiau** and continues downstream where a walkway leads to the **bellstone.**

A couple of miles up the hill,

still on the same road (580) is the scenic viewpoint for **'Ōpaeka'a Falls.** On the opposite side of this bridge, there is a splendid view of the **Wailua River** and the tour boats going to and from the **Fern Grotto,** a pretty, fern-encrusted cavern farther upstream. The grotto's flowers and ferns grow upside down from the top of the cave, and after a look inside, visitors are serenaded with the 'Hawaiian Wedding Song'. It is also, as the song suggests, a popular site for weddings. From the bridge, you also look down upon **Kamokila Hawaiian Village,** an excellent reconstructed facsimile of the village that once stood on the site; the entrance to Kamokila is immediately adjacent to the western *(mauka)* end of the bridge.

Nounou Ridge, the mountain spur behind Wailua has the profile of a reclining man and is known in legend as the **Sleeping Giant.** North of Wailua, Kūhiō Highway (56) passes the huge Market Place at Coconut Plantation on the edge of Waipouli before entering Kapa'a, the largest town on the island. At the north end of town, there is a scenic lookout over **Keālia Bay.** Between here and the north shore are a lot of cane fields. About halfway between **Anahola Bay** and **Moloa'a Bay,** there is a scenic lookout, and at the Moloa'a Road turnoff, there is an excellent fruit stand well worth a stop.

Several miles farther along Kūhiō Highway, you come to the small town of **Kīlauea.** Perpendicular to a charming little lava rock church, Christ Memorial Episcopal Church, is Kīlauea Road. Traveling along this road, you'll pass the attractive **Kong Lung Co.** store, a very old store, established in 1892, with upscale clothes, furniture and unique gifts.

Princeville has private homes, condos and golf courses.

At the end of Kīlauea Road is the picturesque **Kīlauea Lighthouse,** built in 1913, within the **Kīlauea Point Wildlife Refuge.** Kaua'i's rugged Kilauea Point is a favored nesting site for large colonies of red-footed boobies, wedge-tailed shearwaters and other species.

Just west of Kīlauea is a scenic lookout over Kalihiwai Bay, followed by the Princeville Airport. A couple of miles farther, on the left, you can't miss the entrance to the Princeville resort community, which contains condominiums and private homes, many available for short-term rentals; two top-ranked golf courses, the Makai Course and the Prince Course; and the **Princeville Hotel.** Immediately past the shopping center, on the opposite side of the road, is a scenic viewpoint providing a stunning vista of the beautiful **Hanalei Valley** and an interesting wildlife exhibit. The road then winds sharply downhill to the picturesque old Hanalei Bridge, thence to Hanalei Town. A little farther westward, at Waioli, are the **Waioli Mission Church,** and, behind it, the **Waioli Mission House.**

From here the road follows the shoreline quite closely, passing many beautiful beaches, and is punctuated at frequent intervals by one-lane bridges over the many small streams running through this well-watered agricultural district. Especially quaint is the double bridge at Wainiha. West of Hā'ena are three ancient lava tubes known as **Maniniholo Dry Cave, Waikapala'e Wet Cave** and **Waikanaloa Wet Cave,** which, according to legend, were dug by the goddess Pele. Geologists prefer to believe that they were formed by wave action when the sea level was higher, some four thousand years ago. At the end of the road is **Kē'ē Beach.** Kē'ē Lagoon offers excellent swimming and snorkeling when waters are calm.

The Fern Grotto has long been a popular wedding site.

Near the path from the beach to the *heiau* is a cottage where part of the movie *The Thornbirds* was filmed. Beside the parking area at the end of the road is a large sign marking the beginning of the Kalalau Trail into the valleys of the **Nā Pali Coast.**

HISTORIC SITES AND BUILDINGS

For ancient Hawaiians, virtually all natural features of the landscape had meaning. In a culture rich with oral tradition, the symbolic significance of every cave, crater, pinnacle and headland was passed from generation to generation, giving life and immediacy to the historic and mythical legends of gods and heroes. This abundant lore fills volumes, but here we offer a sampling to provide a glimpse of the way the Hawaiians of old related to the land that nurtured them.

Kaua'i's folklore is especially rich with tales of the *Menehune* (see INTRODUCTION), and these tiny people are held responsible for many of the natural features of the land-scape as well as for some otherwise unexplained man-made structures. The most outstanding and well known of the latter are **Kīkī a Ola** or the **Menehune Ditch** at Waimea and **Alakoko** or the **Menehune Fishpond** on the Hulē'ia River at Niumalu. Kīkī a Ola was an irrigation canal that brought water from high in the Waimea Canyon to the taro patches of the ancient village of Waimea. The cut and keyed stonemasonry demonstrates both knowledge and tools of a technology the Hawaiians of Cook's day did not have, so the artisans' identity remains a mystery. This sort of stonework is found nowhere else in the Hawaiian Islands. Alakoko is a 900-foot-long wall cutting off a bend

Waimea Canyon, early morning

in the river to create an enormous pond for raising and harvesting fish. Such ponds were common along the coasts of all Hawaiian islands, but the size of the stonework of this one is exceptional.

Pōhaku Ho'ohānau or the **Royal Birthing Stones,** located near Holoholokū Heiau in Wailua, is a consecrated grouping of large stones where *ali'i* women were brought to give birth ceremonially, with the appropriate *kahuna* in attendance, in order to assure the highest *mana* for their offspring. If the newborn were male, the nearby **bellstone** was rung; females entered the world unannounced.

The mountain ridge behind Wailua is the form of a **Sleeping Giant** named **Nounou.** He sleeps for centuries at a time and gets all covered with dirt, and trees grow on him. People forget about him and have, it is said, been very frightened when he wakes, but he is a friendly fellow who has helped the local people with such tasks as transporting stones from one side of the island to the other and building *heiau*. Exhausted from his labors and full after a feast given in celebration of his last completed work, he lay down again for another few centuries of deep slumber.

The fire goddess Pele is said to have come north from the land of Kahiki in search of a new home. Her route of migration took her right across the Hawaiian Islands, and everywhere she went, she thrust her digging stick into the ground looking for an appropriate homesite. On Kaua'i's north shore are the results of three unsuccessful attempts—**Maniniholo Dry Cave, Waikapala'e Wet Cave** and **Waikanaloa Wet Cave**—before she moved on across the archipelago,

finally finding what she was looking for in the Big Island's Kīlauea Firepit, where she still lives and regularly reminds residents of her presence.

There are also sites of more recent historic interest. Near Ku'unaka'iole Point at Hanapēpē are the ancient **Salt Ponds** where Hawaiians flooded clay beds with sea water and, after evaporation, collected the crystals. They still do, and posted *kapu* signs warn intruders to keep their distance. Locals much prefer the flavor of this salt, red from the residue of clay it contains, over the commercial variety, but it cannot be sold as it does not meet government standards of purity. A park on Lāwa'i Road between Kōloa and Kukui'ula (the route to Spouting Horn) marks the birthplace of Prince Jonah Kūhiō Kalaniana'ole, born on March 26, 1871, to High Chief David Kahalepouli Pi'ikoi and Kinoiki Kekaulike. After the over-throw of the Hawaiian monarchy, Kūhiō served as Hawai'i's second elected representative in Washington, DC from 1902 until his death on January 7, 1922.

On the north bank of the Wailua River, a couple of miles upstream from the ocean, stood a village whose remains were uncovered in the 1930s by a farmer, Ben Ohai. Aware of the significance of the site and of the fading of Hawaiian culture, he made it his life's work to excavate and recreate that village as an educational site. Though he did not live to see the dream realized, his family has carried it out and the village, now named **Kamokila,** meaning 'stronghold', offers Kaua'i visitors and residents alike the closest thing they're ever likely to see to an ancient Hawaiian village. For those who have visited remote villages on South Pacific islands, where Polynesian culture still thrives, Kamokila Hawaiian Village feels like a time warp, its authenticity a palpable presence. Demonstrations of food preparation, crafts and ancient games are also included. (Mon.-Sat. 9:00 a.m.-4:00 p.m., admission $8/adults, $5/children ages 6-12, 822-1192)

At the mouth of the Waimea River stands the ruins of **Fort Elizabeth,** built by Russians in 1816 in an unsuccessful attempt to gain a foothold in the islands, serving as a strategic and secure base of supply for their outposts in Alaska and the northwest coast of North America. The plans of Dr. George Anton Scheffer, their commercial agent, who carried out this scheme, were disavowed by the Tsar, and Kaumuali'i, still ruler of the island, was chastised by Kamehameha I, to whom he had pledged his loyalty. The wall of the fort originally sloped directly to the river, but subsequent siltation has created a ledge in front of it.

Kilohana was built in 1935 by Gaylord and Ethel Wilcox of Grove Farm Plantation, one of Kaua'i's largest sugar growers. Unoccupied and unattended for many years, the home has now been restored and converted to commercial use except in the living room and dining room, which have been retained with their furnishings, many of them the originals, to illustrate the gracious lifestyle of the former residents.

George Wilcox founded Grove Farm Plantation in 1864, and ran it from **Grove Farm Homestead.** The original plantation house, added on to in later years, is still there, along with the plantation office, guest and workers' cottages, work sheds, flower and vegetable gardens, fruit orchards and more. The Wilcox family occupied this home continuously for more than a century, until Miss Mabel Wilcox, who was born on the property, died in 1978 at the age of 96. Prior to her death she planned the present use of her 80-acre estate, establishing a non-profit educational organization to maintain Grove Farm

The ruins of Russian Fort Elizabeth.

Homestead and Waioli Mission House, and to preserve, study and interpret the history of missionary and plantation life on Kaua'i. Miss Wilcox and her sisters also collected, over the period of their lifetimes, an outstanding collection of Hawaiian quilts, which have been preserved in exceptionally good condition and are kept at Grove Farm. A beautifully illustrated book—*The Wilcox Quilts in Hawaii*—describing these, the people who made them and the people who collected them, is available at the office.

Mabel Wilcox and her sisters, Ethel Wilcox and Etta Sloggett, are also responsible for the preservation and restoration, in 1921, of **Waioli Mission House** at Waioli, near Hanalei. It is the former home of their grandparents, Abner and Lucy Wilcox, missionary teachers who came to Kaua'i in 1846. Shipped around Cape Horn from Boston in 1836, in pre-cut pieces, this typical two-story New England cottage was erected by Reverend William Alexander, Kaua'i's first missionary preacher, and was subsequently occupied by the Wilcox family until it became a museum. Much of the original furniture was and still is in it, preserving the flavor of 19th-century missionary life in this remote corner. (T, Th., Sat., 9:00 a.m.-3:00 p.m., admission free, 245-3202).

The 52-foot **Kīlauea Lighthouse,** built in 1913, boasts the world's largest clamshell lens, the moving parts of which weigh four tons. An electronic beacon, installed in front of the lighthouse in 1976, has superseded the massive lamp, which completed a revolution every twenty seconds, turning on a mercury float, and flashing ten thousand candlepower seaward every ten seconds. Still operated by the U.S. Coast Guard, the lighthouse is now within the Kīlauea Point Wildlife Refuge (grounds open M-F, 10:00 a.m.-4:00 p.m.; scenic overlook provides view at all times).

MUSEUMS

The **Kōke'e Natural History Museum,** located next to Kōke'e Lodge in Kōke'e State Park houses displays of the plant and animal life of Kaua'i and the other Hawaiian islands, an excellent three-dimensional map of Kaua'i, and a fascinating exhibit on Hawai'i's hurricanes, featuring 1992's Hurricane Iniki.

A permanent exhibit at the **Kaua'i Museum** tells the story of Kaua'i—or as much of it as is known—from its formation as a single volcanic island some sixty million years ago, up un-til the 19th century and the development of the sugar plantations. An excellent continuous loop film gives an overview of Kaua'i today; ask at the desk about purchasing a cassette of its superb sound track. Another wing of the museum houses local artifacts and temporary exhibitions, generally of very high quality, that change every few months. The Museum Shop carries a very good selection of books and gift items related to the natural and cultural history of the island (M-F, 9:00 a.m.-4:30 p.m., Sat. 9:00 a.m.-1:00 p.m., 4428 Rice Street, Lihue, 245-6931, admission $3/adults, children under 18 free).

The **Hawaiian Art Museum** in Kīlauea (2488 Kolo Rd.) exhibits arts and crafts by local artists, and has a bookstore which sells a wide range of maps and books about Hawai'i.

HEIAU

The sacred structures where Hawaiians ceremonially honored their gods are known as *heiau*. The remains of many of these can be seen, though some have been completely destroyed in the clearing of land for alternate use, and others are shrouded in dense thickets of overgrowth. Though official use of all *heiau* ceased more than a century ago, fresh offerings are often found at the ruins. As these sites are still considered sacred by many of Hawai'i's people, please treat them with due respect, keeping them clean and leaving all stones in place.

Those *heiau* most likely to be encountered by visitors are in the Wailua area, the seat of power for Kaua'i's ruling chiefs before European contact. At the mouth of the Wailua River, on the south bank in a coconut grove lie the ruins of **Hikini a Kalā Heiau** and, adjacent to it, those of **Hau'ola Pu'uhonua,** an ancient place of refuge for offenders who had broken *kapu*, or warriors who had been defeated in battle. If they could reach a *pu'uhonua* (place of peace and safety) before their pursuers could catch them, they were safe and, after a period of time, could return to society. Beside the river are several boulders carved with ancient petroglyphs; these are sometimes covered with sand and difficult to detect. Just mauka of Kūhiō Highway (56), on Kuamo'o Road (580) lie the ruins of **Holoholokū Heiau**. This former *luakini* is on the left, right beside the road. The stone slab in the far corner was the sacrificial altar.

Only a few yards farther along the roadside are the Pōhaku Ho'ohānau or the **Royal Birthing Stones**, a consecrated site where *ali'i* women gave birth. Farther up Kuamo'o Road on the left hand side, shortly before the lookout for 'Ōpaeka'a Falls, a dirt road leads to the ruins of **Poli'ahu Heiau** and continues downstream where a walkway leads to the **bellstone,** one of a group of boulders, which, when struck precisely at a particular spot, gives a clear ringing tone. According to tradition, the bellstone was sounded to announce the birth of male *ali'i* at the *pōhaku ho'ohānau* down the hill. It is not now known which of the stones was used or how to tap it to produce a sound that carries for an appreciable distance. Many people try their hand, however, and as a result, the stones have been badly damaged and are being gradually chipped away. Visitors to the site are asked to refrain from hitting the stones.

The other important *heiau* in the area, **Malae Heiau,** is in the middle of a cane field and all overgrown so it cannot, at present, be visited with ease. There are two other *heiau* in accessible places. On the south shore, **Kihahōuna Heiau** sits right on Po'ipū Beach, in front of the Waiohai Hotel and slightly to the east; it can also be reached from the west via Po'ipū Beach Park.

On the north shore above Kē'ē Beach, which lies at the very end of the road, stand the ruins of **Kaulu Paoa Heiau** and, above that, the ancient site of a *halau* (hula school). The hula platform at this site is still used by local *halau*, and is regularly cleaned and maintained by them.

Offerings left at Hau'ola Pu'uhonua

PARKS AND GARDENS

Nā Pali Coast State Park encompasses some of the significant eastern valleys of the Nā Pali Coast wilderness. The best known of the valleys is **Kalalau,** east of Nu'alolo, where the remains of terracing and irrigation are most extensive. This wide valley ends at a long, lovely beach, in summer; much of the sand is removed by raging winter surf and redeposited each spring. Access to Kalalau is also possible by an arduous eleven-mile trail that snakes its way up and down along a ledge hugging the cliffs. Built by Hawaiians many centuries ago, the trail is very popular today with hikers and backpackers, but it is not for the casual stroller or the faint of heart. Starting from the end of the road at Ka'ilio Point, the trail passes through two other large valleys on its way to Kalalau—**Hanakāpī'ai** and **Hanakoa.** The former is two miles along the trail, a steep mile up and a steep mile down. At the back of this valley is a splendid 300-foot waterfall.

The second valley is four miles farther along, the trail passing through a couple of small valleys— Ho'olulu and Waiahuakua—along the way. Hanakoa, a very rainy place, also has a lovely waterfall. Another five miles of steep, narrow trail, passing through another small valley called Pōhakuao, bring the intrepid adventurer at last to Kalalau Valley, with its pools, falls, ancient ruins and abundant legends, perhaps the favorite of which is that of Ko'olau the Leper.

A native of Kekaha on Kaua'i's south shore, Ko'olau contracted leprosy and in 1889 was scheduled for transportation to the Kalaupapa settlement on Moloka'i. As the boat set sail without his wife and child, whom he was promised could accompany him, Ko'olau realized that he had been tricked and jumped overboard, swimming ashore. With his family he hid in Kalalau where a number of lepers sought to evade the authorities. After a year, all the lepers in the valley were persuaded to leave, except Ko'olau, who outmaneuvered a sheriff's posse and a subsequent detachment of the National Guard, killing or wounding several of them in the process. Left alone, Ko'olau and his wife (their son also contracted the disease and died quickly) lived in the valley for another five years until he died and she buried him there. Ko'olau has become something of a local folk hero.

The hanging valleys, ending in sheer cliffs at the sea, which lie farther westward along this coast, are now described as 'inaccessible', but they were inhabited and extensively terraced by large groups of Hawaiians in the many centuries of occupation prior to the arrival of Europeans in the islands. As the culture and values changed, the difficulty of access to these valleys became a burden and they were abandoned, but remains of lo'i (taro terraces), irrigation channels, *heiau* and house foundations are still evident beneath the overgrowth.

The largest population, sometimes dramatically referred to as the 'lost tribe', occupied three large valleys—**Honopū, Awa'awapuhi** and **Nu'alolo**—and six smaller ones. At Nu'alolo there is a beach below the sheer cliffs where canoes landed. Access to the valley above was by means of a rope ladder. There was also a permanent settlement known as Nu'alolo Kai (the valley above

Nu'alolo 'Aina) nestled against the cliffs at the back of the beach, and the stone remains of this village can be visited by boat. The beach area is now **Nu'alolo Kai State Park**. A little farther westward along the coast is another beach, **Miloli'i State Park,** below the Koahole Valley and accessible only by private boat.

A few miles down the west coast of the island is **Polihale State Park,** a hot, dry area popular for its long sandy beach and sunset views, the color dramatically reflected by the high, rocky cliffs in the background. The area was special to the Hawaiians of old, and the park contains the ruins of two large *heiau*—**Kapā'ula**

Canyon State Park and are contiguous with **Kōke'e State Park,** encompassing 4345 acres of the island's upland wilderness and affording unsurpassed opportunities for exploring an unspoiled natural environment. The parks' nature trails vary greatly in length and difficulty, offering something for everyone. Adjacent to Kōke'e State Park is the **Alaka'i Wilderness Preserve,** encompassing the Alaka'i Swamp, which, at ten miles long and two miles wide, is approximately the size and shape of Manhattan. Entry into the swamp's upper reaches is restricted, but hiking into parts of it is permitted. Altogether there are 45

A rainbow arcs down to the Waimea mountains.

Heiau and **Polihale Heiau**—a sacred spring. Access is from the end of the highway via five miles of graded dirt road, which can become impassable for ordinary cars in very wet weather.

Around the curve of the island on the south coast is the mouth of Waimea Canyon, stretching twelve miles up into the island's interior. Some 1866 acres of the chasm's upper reaches are designated **Waimea**

miles of wonderful nature trails—for both vehicles and hiking—in this area.

For the casual stroller, the delights of nature can be enjoyed at one of Kaua'i's several botanical gardens. **'Olu Pua Gardens and Plantation Estate,** off Kaumuali'i Highway one mile west of Kalāheo, was founded in the 1900s as a plantation manager's estate of the Kaua'i Pineapple Company. Its twelve and a half acres have been converted to a private botanical garden with an active, ongoing collecting program to expand the diversity of plants, which already include tropical vegetation from around the world. Hour-long narrated tours of the grounds are given five times a day and provide ample information about the many types of trees, flowers, vines, shrubs and other plants. (The grounds are open daily 9:00 a.m.-3:00 p.m., with guided tours from 9:30 a.m. to 1:30 p.m.; admission $10/adults, $5/ children under 12; call 332-8182 for reservations. Closed Christmas and New Year's Day.)

Kaua'i's 186-acre **National Trop-** **ical Botanical Garden,** dedicated in 1971, was chartered by the U.S. Congress as a tropical plant research center, the primary function of which is the increase of scientific knowledge. The world's tropics contain vast numbers of unstudied species, even undescribed species, and new ones are continually being discovered.

Since the garden's Visitor Center was destroyed by Hurricane Iniki, a new center is currently under construction and, as of this writing, has not yet opened, so please call to obtain information. Reservations are required for tours (two hours long), which also include the gardens of the

49

Late afternoon sun shadows the Nā Pali Coast.

adjacent Allerton estate, an exquisite haven started in the 1870s by Queen Emma, wife of Kamehameha IV. (Tour M-F: $20/person, reservations/ information - 332-7361)

Smith's Tropical Paradise is spread across 30 acres along the south bank of the Wailua River, with its entrance next to the Wailua Marina, and is a good choice for families. Attractively landscaped, it offers a suggested route or you may find your own way amongst the labeled exotic specimens of native and introduced tropical foliage with pseudo-Polynesian and Filipino structures and a huge head meant to resemble those stone monoliths from Easter Island scattered about for added interest. A garden in the middle of the pond is graced by a Japanese garden. A lu'au is held here Mondays, Wednesdays and Fridays from 5:00 to 9:00 p.m. with an international show in the amphi-theater. Trams run at night, at a cost

of $1.00 per person. A free shuttle service is available from the Wailua area. (Open daily 8:30 a.m.-4:00 p.m., admission: $5/adults, $2.50/children under 11; luau and show: $43.75/ adults, $26/children - 822-4654 for luau or shuttle reservations)

At Po'ipū Beach, the **Kiahuna Plantation Resort and Gardens,** is well worth a stroll-through. The estate boasts 4,000 species of plants, including Hawaiian orchids, and is listed in the book *Great Gardens of America*. Sustaining extensive damage from 1992's destructive Hurricane Iniki, the resort reopened in October, 1994. Its spectacular grounds were once part of the oldest sugar cane plantation in Hawai'i, and include 35 landscaped acres of lawn, a lagoon, lily ponds, tropical flowers and fruit trees and a world famous cactus garden. (2253 Po'ipū Rd., 742-6411)

Kaua'i's only pineapple garden, located in Līhu'e, may be viewed free

The clouds' dramatic unveiling of Kalalau Valley.

of charge at **Kaua'i Fruit & Flower Co.,** which features 21 varieties from around the world. Packaged pineapples and papayas are available for purchase, for delivery on the island or shipping elsewhere (3-4684 Kūhiō Hwy.; Mon.-Sat. 8:00 a.m.- 4:00 p.m. - 245-1814).

Wailua River State Park encompasses 1126 acres of the Wailua River and its banks up the South Fork to Wailua Falls and up the North Fork past 'Ōpaeka'a Falls to Koholālele Falls, including **Lydgate State Park** on the coast near the Kauai Resort Hotel. The River Park contains the remains of several *heiau* and other culturally important sites as well as the popular tourist destination, the Fern Grotto. The Beach Park contains the ruins of a *heiau* and associated *pu'uhonua.*

Kīlauea Point National Wildlife Refuge on Kaua'i's rugged Kīlauea Point is a nesting site for large colonies of red-footed boobies and wedge-tailed shearwaters; and other species such as the red-tailed tropic bird, the Laysan albatross and the great frigate bird are also seen here. A Visitor Center adjacent to Kīlauea Lighthouse as of this writing is closed for remodeling, after incurring damage in Hurricane Iniki in 1992. When it reopens, it will feature displays explaining Hawai'i's seabird sanctuaries and the birds they protect.

Hā'ena State Park, a 62-acre beach park on the north coast, where camping is extremely popular, is detailed in BEACHES and ACCOMMODATION.

Polihale Beach, still considered a sacred place by many.

Crystal clear Hā'ena Point.

BEACHES

Kaua'i is blessed with sweeping strands of pristine sand along most of its coast. Ocean recreation was an important facet of life for the ancient Hawaiians, and remains a major feature of island life for visitors as well as residents. Many island visitors come from inland areas and are unfamiliar with the awesome power of the sea, with the vagaries of its personality. For all its beauty, it must be approached with respect and caution; and then it provides a great deal of pleasure. This section contains information relevant to beach activity--including warnings--followed by descriptions and ratings of Kaua'i's beaches.

WARNINGS

Heed all warning signs posted at beaches. Lifeguards are stationed at only six of Kaua'i's beaches--Kē'ē, Hanalei, Po'ipū, Salt Pond, Wailua and Lydgate--and many of this island's beaches are steep and have very strong ocean currents, especially in winter when high surf is usual. Recorded information on current surf conditions around the island is available at 246-4441, code 1521, a service provided by GTE Hawaiian Tel.

Many visitors spoil their vacations by spending too much time in the sun the first day or two. The sun in Hawai'i is much harsher than in more northerly (or quite southerly) climes, primarily due to the thinner ozone layer and direct angle of the sun at this latitude. A sunblock with an SPF of 30 or greater is recommended for all skin tones. Limit your sun exposure the first few days so as not to overdo it. You can increase your sun exposure in gradual increments as you develop a tan. Remember to take along some bottled water to cool yourself off and prevent dehydration.

One of the gravest potential dangers of the deep is the caprice of waves. 'Typical' wave action varies with the local shoreline and the season. On Kaua'i's north shore, the sheer size of the winter surf is dangerous, with waves cresting up to thirty feet. The surf on the eastern and western shorelines can also be high in winter. In summer, high seasonal surf can occur off the south shore.

Shorebreaks are places on or near the shore, where incoming ocean swells cross abruptly from a deep to a shallow bottom and the waves break with enormous downward force. Though they are dangerous for swimmers, these beaches are popular as they provide excellent conditions for body surfing. It is well, though, to know how to deal with them. Neck and back injuries can be sustained, and turning your back on or trying to jump over or through a large incoming wave invites trouble. The force of the wave can pound you against the bottom, knock your breath away and cause you to lose your sense of direction. The trick is to take a deep breath and dive *under* the wave.

Another potential danger at such beaches is the backwash, water which has been washed onto the shore and must run back again to the sea. On steep beaches, or after the arrival of particularly voluminous waves, the force of this water can be almost as powerful as the incoming wave and can sweep a person off his or her feet and out to deeper water.

This water rushing back to the sea sometimes gets trapped by other incoming waves and can build to a considerable volume. When this happens, the only way it can move is sideward, creating a rip current that runs along the beach until it finds a deeper bottom. If you find yourself caught in a rip, the best course of action is to flow along with it until its force diminishes. Don't exhaust yourself trying to swim against it. It's easier and safer to walk back along the beach to the place where you started than to fight the water. Some rip currents flow straight out to sea through channels in the reef. If you are caught in one of these, swim to the side of it and get out. This type of rip is far more dangerous.

Sometimes this backed-up water cannot find an outlet and must flow back out *under* the incoming wave.

This creates the condition known as undertow. An undertow is a brief phenomenon, lasting only until the wave has passed. For a person pulled down in an undertow, a few seconds under water can seem much longer. Remain calm and come up for air on the other side of the wave.

Another potentially dangerous wave action is the collision of deep ocean swells with rock ledges. It is never safe to venture out to the edge of rocks where surf is breaking. Freak waves can wash over the rocks without warning and many unsuspecting people have been swept away by such waves.

Underwater ledges, too, can present some danger from the surprise of a sudden dropping away of the bottom. Very shallow water can become very deep without notice, so non-swimmers should always keep away from such areas.

RATINGS

We have rated the beaches according to our interpretation of the following criteria: water safety, bottom configuration (sand, rock, coral), cleanliness/maintenance of beach area, and type and quality of facilities (restrooms, showers, picnic tables, barbecue pits, parking). This is naturally arbitrary and not everyone feels the same about what's most important in a beach. All of Kaua'i's beaches are beautiful, though many are washed by very strong currents. Symbols denote beaches that are especially good for board surfing ●, body surfing ● (includes body boarding), windsurfing ●, snorkeling ●, and swimming ●. Seasonal variances are also noted. These are VERY impor-

tant, as they relate primarily to safety.

The ratings and descriptions of beaches are arranged in geographical order around the island in a counter-clockwise direction, starting on the western shore.

Superb	☆☆☆☆
Excellent	☆☆☆
Good	☆☆
Fair	☆

Note: "L" in heading of beach description designates a lifeguard on duty.

54

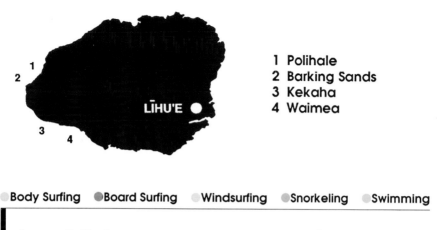

1 Polihale
2 Barking Sands
3 Kekaha
4 Waimea

LĪHU'E ●

● Body Surfing ● Board Surfing ● Windsurfing ● Snorkeling ● Swimming

1   Polihale ★★ ● *(winter, expert only)*

Fringing the edge of Polihale State Park is a wide expanse of white sand that stretches unbroken all the way to Kekaha, about ten miles. The park is at the very end of the road, the last five miles of which are unpaved and bumpy, traversing sugar cane fields. The Nā Pali Coast starts (or ends) here. Above the beach tower spectacular gray cliffs. Ni'ihau and Lehua can be seen on the horizon, and here the sun sets directly into the sea. Unobstructed by fringing reefs, the waves roll in with full force, making even summer water conditions unsafe for swimmers, and the severe winter surf is recommended only for expert surfers. There is a natural pool called **Queen's Bath** about midway down the Park's shoreline, south of the parking lot, which affords safe summer swimming. *Follow the State Park signs from the end of Kaumuali'i Hwy (50). Showers, restrooms, pavilion and barbecue. Tent camping allowed with state permit.*

2   Barking Sands ★

This wide, sandy beach has surf and water conditions similar to those at Polihale. Public use of the beach at the Barking Sands Missile Range is allowed when there are no military maneuvers in progress (call 335-4111). *Access is through the military reserve and visitors must sign in at the gate.*

3   Kekaha ★★★ ●●●

This long, wide stretch of sand along the southwest coast is a continuation of the beach that starts beneath the cliffs at Polihale. Though it is subject to strong rip currents and surf from both southern summer and western winter storms, it can have safe, calm conditions at any time of year (call the surf report at 246-4441, code 1521). *Access is directly off Kaumuali'i Hwy. (50). Restrooms, pavilion and barbecue are across highway from the beach.*

Building sand castles, a favorite beach pastime

4   Waimea   ● (summer)

What has been erroneously called Waimea Black Sand Beach in some guidebooks is really just a muddy shoreline. The sand is black from dirt washed down the Waimea River and is not volcanic black sand, as are some of the beaches on the Big Island. The water is also murky with suspended soil particles, making swimming conditions poor. The fishing pier here is very popular and there is good summer surfing offshore. *Turn makai just west of the Waimea River Bridge.*

5   Pākalā   ☆   ●● (summer)

Located off the main highway and reached via a path through a cane field, this secluded curve of sand, rendered bronze by runoff from the rich red earth beyond, is divided by a rocky promontory. The water is shallow and murky from soil runoff, and the bottom is rocky, making swimming conditions unpleasant. The offshore surfing break here, known as **Infinities,** is considered one of the best summer surfing spots in all Hawai'i, for experts only. *Park beside Kaumuali'i Hwy. (50) on a wide sandy area beside a low concrete bridge shortly past mile marker 21.*

6   Salt Pond Beach Park   ☆☆☆☆   ●●   L

This is the perfect spot for a family outing. A semicircular band of gently sloping golden sand and a protective fringing reef make this one of the island's most popular swimming beaches. Persistent patterns of fair weather add to its appeal. Large protected pools at either end of the beach provide safe "baby pools" for young children to splash around in. Lifeguards are on duty daily, year-round. During high surf conditions, currents can be strong, and swimmers are advised to stay within the lagoon. Some of the ancient salt pans nearby are still used by locals to harvest sea salt, and tidal pools harbor interesting little sea creatures. *At Hanapēpē, turn makai at the sign pointing to the Veterans Cemetery, then take the first right onto Lokokai Road and proceed to the parking area. Showers, restrooms, picnic tables and barbecues available.*

7   Po'ipū Beach Park   ☆☆☆☆   ●●●●   (summer)   L

Another fairly long stretch of wide, sandy shoreline with a sloping sandy bottom, this is generally a good swimming beach, with stronger wave surges in summer providing bodysurfing conditions. Lifeguards are on duty daily year-round, and anyone is free to use the beaches fronting the hotels. An area past a rocky point at the eastern end of the beach, generally known as Brennecke's, makes the area dangerous for any wave riding. *Follow Maluhia Road (520) or Kōloa Road (530) to Kōloa Town, then take Po'ipū Road makai to the coast. Showers, restrooms, picnic tables, pavilions, barbecues, children's playground.*

● Body Surfing ● Board Surfing ● Windsurfing ● Snorkeling ● Swimming

8   Shipwreck (Keoneloa) Beach   ☆ ●● (summer)

This pretty stretch of unshaded beach is washed by strong currents and surf. Fringed by a rocky shelf that spoils it as a swimming beach, some body surfers and boogie boarders use it in summer, and it is popular year-round with windsurfers. *Access is via a dirt road between the Hyatt and the Po'ipū Bay Resort golf course. To get to the dirt road, turn left at the end of the paved portion of Po'ipū Road, then turn right (makai) at the first opportunity. Note: the outdoor showers near the beach are designated for Hyatt guests only.*

9   Māhā'ulepū   ☆☆ ●●

Though all beaches in Hawai'i are public up to the high-water mark, land access to this lovely stretch of shaded sand is possible only by crossing privately owned land. The western end is protected by a fringing reef, however swimming and snorkeling can be hazardous during the summertime and off and on throughout the year when strong currents and a high surf are present. This beach is best for exploring, as there are picturesque rock formations and interesting tide pools. Don't be tempted to climb on the rocks, as waves can crash upon them suddenly and unexpectedly. *On Po'ipū road, past the Hyatt Hotel and past Shipwreck Beach, you will come to a stop sign. Turn right (makai) and stop at the gatehouse, where you will need to sign a release form to cross through sugar plantation land. Follow the road to the end, where you may turn right or left.*

10   Kīpū Kai   ☆☆☆ ●●

Accessible only by water, this pretty, isolated beach with a gently sloping sandy bottom is a favorite spot for boat outings, particularly during winter when high surf conditions prevent the popular boat trips down the Nā Pali Coast (see 'Water Tours' under GETTING AROUND).

11   Kalapakī   ☆☆☆ ●●●● (summer)

This is the 'town beach', in front of the Kaua'i Marriott and adjacent to Nāwiliwili County Park. The beachfront has a gently sloping sandy bottom and the sheltered cove affords good swimming, windsurfing, boogie boarding and body surfing all year and, occasionally in summer, even board surfing. *At the bottom of Wa'apā Road, Līhu'e. Picnic facilities available at Nāwiliwili Park.*

12   Hanamā'ulu   ☆ ●

The beach here is a crescent of soft sand, with a gradually sloping sandy bottom, but Hanamā'ulu Stream, which empties into the bay, makes the water murky and poor for water activity. There are restrooms, showers and picnic facilities, and the area is popular for camping. *Turn makai off Kūhiō Hwy (56) at Hanama'ulu, bear right at the fork and follow the road to the end.*

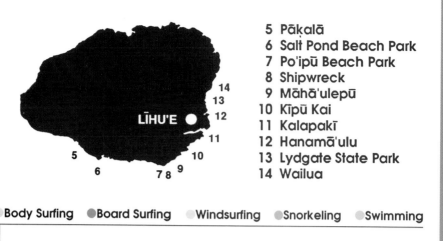

5 Pākalā
6 Salt Pond Beach Park
7 Po'ipū Beach Park
8 Shipwreck
9 Māhā'ulepū
10 Kīpū Kai
11 Kalapakī
12 Hanamā'ulu
13 Lydgate State Park
14 Wailua

● Body Surfing   ● Board Surfing   ● Windsurfing   ● Snorkeling   ● Swimming

13   Lydgate State Park   ★★★   ●● L

Though this stretch of coastline is subject to strong currents and dangerous winter surf, lava walls have been built at this popular beach park to
break the force of the waves, creating two areas (one shallow enough for
small children) that are are safe for swimming all year. When the sea is
calm, snorkeling is good outside the breakwater, but powerful currents at the
river mouth make swimming here risky at all times. The park has all the

Hanalei, awash in the blushing glow of sunset skies

● Body Surfing ● Board Surfing ● Windsurfing ● Snorkeling ● Swimming

facilities for family outings, and interesting ruins of a *heiau* and *pu'uhonua* lie in the coconut grove. *Access is off Leho Drive, which is a loop that joins Kūhiō Hwy (56) just north of the Wailua Golf Course and just south of the Kaua'i Resort Hotel. Restrooms, showers, picnic area provided.*

14   Wailua   ★★   ●● (winter)   L

Unprotected by fringing reef, this stretch of wide, sandy beach is washed by strong currents all year and, in winter when ocean swells run higher, the area is popular for surfing, but water conditions for swimmers are quite dangerous. *Access directly from Kūhiō Hwy (56), across from Coco Palms Resort.*

15   Kapa'a   ★   ●

A small reef about twenty yards offshore protects the Kapa'a shoreline from the full force of ocean swells, but the beaches are eroded and narrow and the bottom shallow and rocky, making swimming conditions poor. Snorkeling is okay in calm conditions. *Access directly off Kūhiō Hwy (56).*

16   Keālia   ★★   ●● (summer, cove only)

A popular surfing spot north of Kapa'a, this long, wide beach has a sheltered cove at the north end where swimming is safe in summer. In high surf, only expert swimmers and surfers should challenge the powerful waves and strong currents. Interesting tide pools at the southern end attract marine biology students as well as the casually curious. *Access directly off Kūhiō Hwy (56).*

17   Donkey Beach   ★★   ●

The private cane roads leading to this isolated beach are no longer available for public access by car. However, this popular 'bathing suit optional' beach is accessible via a short walk from the road by requesting a permit from Līhu'e Plantation, whose office is at 2970 Kele Street in Līhu'e, next to the Post Office. Although a favorite surfing spot, water conditions and strong currents make swimming dangerous. *Three quarters of a mile north of mile marker 11 on the Kūhiō Hwy (56), watch for cars parked roadside. A well-travelled path through a cane field will lead you to the beach.*

18   Anahola Bay   ★★★   ●● (summer)   ●● (winter)

At the eastern end of the bay, Anahola Beach Park has showers, restrooms, picnic tables and barbecues, and a protecting reef offshore makes water conditions safe for summer swimming, but high winter surf can create surges and currents hazardous to swimmers. Winter wave conditions are strongest around the center of the beach with gentler surf at the northern end. This is a favorite beach of local families, and large shallow pools formed where the Anahola Stream meets the bay are popular swimming holes for children.

15 Kapaʻa
16 Keālia
17 Donkey Beach
18 Anahola Bay
19 Moloaʻa Bay
20 Larson's Beach
21 Kīlauea Bay
22 Kauapea
23 Kalihiwai Bay
24 ʻAnini

⬤Body Surfing ⬤Board Surfing ⬤Windsurfing ⬤Snorkeling ⬤Swimming

19 Moloaʻa Bay ★★★ ⬤⬤ (summer)

Tucked into the northeastern edge of the island, this bay is off the beaten path, reached by a winding rural road. The long, wide beach is fronted by a fairly steep sandy bottom, and during heavy surf, there are dangerous currents. *Kūhiō Hwy (56) to Moloaʻa Sunrise Fruit Stand, just south of Kīlauea; left on Kuamoʻo Road, then right on Moloaʻa Road to the end; walk along the path, crossing the shallow stream.*

20 Larsen's Beach ★

Though there is an offshore fringing reef, this beach has amongst the most treacherous water conditions on the island and swimming here at any time is risky, and in winter is out of the question. There are no lifeguards on duty. This beach is, though, a beautiful isolated spot, and is favored by beachcombers and *limu* (seaweed) pickers. *Access is off Koʻolau Road which joins Kūhiō Hwy (56) at both ends. The turn is makai onto a dirt road which is about a mile from either end; the beach access is marked. Cross the cattle guard and follow the trail (about a five-minute walk) downhill to the beach.*

21 Kīlauea Bay ★ ⬤ (winter) ⬤ (summer)

Difficult to get to, Kilauea Bay has a shallow sandy bottom and is safe for swimming on very calm days in summer, but treacherous in winter when high surf rolls right in. *Access is via a long, badly rutted dirt road off Kīlauea Lighthouse Road, the second right past the Kong Lung Co. store. To get to the beach, you must wade across Kīlauea Stream, shallow at low tide. Use caution, as high water after a heavy storm makes crossing the stream prohibitive.*

22 Kauapea (Secret Beach) ★ ⬤⬤ (winter) ⬤ (summer)

So far off the beaten path that it is referred to locally as 'Secret Beach', this secluded stretch of sand is the island's foremost nudist beach. Lying at the base of a cliff just west of Kīlauea Point, it can be reached only by a brief hike (about 10 minutes). Wide in summer, the beach may almost disappear under the pounding waves of winter surf. Currents are unpredictable. *Access is*

61

●Body Surfing ●Board Surfing ○Windsurfing ●Snorkeling ○Swimming

via a dirt road just a few yards west of Kolo Road (the entrance to Kīlauea Town); turn makai off Kūhiō Hwy (56) and follow the road until it ends. A sign marks the beginning of the beach trail.

23   Kalihiwai Bay   ☆☆   ○● (summer)   ● (winter)

This lovely curved bay with a shallow, sandy bottom offers calm and gentle waters in summer and formidable high surf in winter, typical of the north shores of all Hawaiian islands. Good boogie boarding and surfing for beginners in summer months, and for experienced surfers in winter months. *There are two separate intersections of Kalihiwai Road with Kūhiō Hwy (56), and although the beach may be reached from either direction, the easternmost entrance is best.*

24   'Anini   ☆☆   ○● (summer)

This county beach park has showers, restrooms, and picnic facilities, and the white sand beach itself stretches for a couple of miles. The water is quite shallow, making it ideal for snorkeling and novice windsurfing, but too shallow for swimming. Even in winter when the rest of the north shore is dangerous, this beach and its inshore waters are sheltered by a fringing reef that is the largest in Hawai'i. Across the street is a polo ground, with matches held on Sunday afternoon in the summer, for a nominal admission fee. *Access is via 'Anini Road, a turn west off the western section of Kalihiwai Road, which runs makai off Kūhiō Hwy (56) almost opposite the Princeville Airport.*

25   Hanalei Bay   ☆☆☆☆   ○● (winter, expert only)   L

This perfect, curved bay, legendary for its beauty, is subject to dangerously strong rip currents and a crashing shorebreak even in summer, especially around the center of the bay, and to raging surf in winter. Swimming here can be dangerous, and it is best to swim at the western end of the bay, where waters tend to be calmer. This is a favorite surfing spot, with surfers from the outer islands flocking here to ride the big waves, which often measure twenty feet in wintertime. *Access is via Aku Road or Weke Road, both makai turns off Kūhiō Hwy (56) at either end of Hanalei Town.*

26   Lumaha'i   ☆☆☆☆   ●● (winter, expert)   ○ (summer, far eastern end only)

This long, wide strip of sandy shoreline is amongst the most beautiful and most photographed beaches in the world. It is best known for its starring role in the movie *South Pacific*. Unfortunately, no fringing reef protects its inshore waters, and the beachfront is totally exposed to the full force of the ocean. Powerful waves and riptides make swimming extremely dangerous except during summer, on days when very calm water conditions permit. *Access at the western end is directly off Kūhiō Hwy (56); at the eastern end of the trail descends a steep, muddy slope (there is no marker, but you will see lots of cars parked along the makai side of the road).*

25 Hanalei Bay
26 Lumaha'i
27 Wainiha
28 Hā'ena
29 Kē'ē
30 Nā Pali

LĪHU'E

●Body Surfing ●Board Surfing ●Windsurfing ●Snorkeling ●Swimming

Sunset fades on Kaua'i's south shore.

●Body Surfing   ●Board Surfing   ●Windsurfing   ●Snorkeling   ●Swimming

27   Wainiha   ☆

This beach is beautiful and usually fairly empty because its steep foreshore and strong currents make water activity here dangerous. It is, nonetheless, an excellent spot for sunning and picnicking in pristine solitude. The Wainiha River flows to the sea at the western end of the beach, making waters murky. *Access is directly off Kūhiō Hwy (56).*

28   Hā'ena   ●● (winter)

There are three distinct sections to the long stretch of Hā'ena Beach, each of which has different inshore conditions. All are popular for windsurfing year-round. Winter conditions afford the best wave jumping and are for experts only. The same goes for board riders of the huge winter waves. **Tunnels**, at the eastern end is wide and sandy, and the bottom sandy with a gentle slope. There are patches of rocky reef in the shallow inshore waters, but there is plenty of room around them for good summer swimming. Winter wave conditions are gentler at this end of the beach. Westward along the beach is **Hā'ena Beach Park,** a popular area for camping. Swimming is dangerous in winter, when surfing is good. The western end is called **Cannons.** A little steeper than the beach at Tunnels, the backwash here is stronger, but swimming is safe on a calm summer day. *Access to Tunnels is via a dirt road, whose turnoff is one-half mile past mile marker 8 on Rt. 560.*

29   Kē'ē   ☆☆☆   ●● (summer)   L

This small, lovely curve of beach is fronted by a gently sloping sandy bottom in fairly shallow water, calm and protected for swimming in summertime. Winter months bring high surf and strong currents, which can create hazardous conditions for water activities. Its surrounding patches of reef provide excellent snorkeling grounds. *This is the end of the road (560); the beach is next to the small parking lot, which also is the starting point for the Kalalau Trail into the valleys of the Nā Pali Coast. If lot is full, continue further on the road, and you can park on the left. Showers and restrooms available.*

30   Nā Pali   ☆   ●● (winter, expert only)

Tucked into the cliffs along this precipitous coastline are beaches at **Hanakāpī'ai** and **Kalalau,** which are accessible via the Kalalau Trail (see 'Hiking' under SPORTS). These are largely ripped away by ocean currents during the high surf of winter and redeposited in spring. Accessible only by boat are the beachheads at **Nu'alolo Kai** and **Miloli'i State Parks** (see 'Water Tours' under GETTING AROUND). *Extreme caution should be exercised at these wilderness beaches, as there is no help nearby in case of emergency.*

64

SPORTS

Scuba Diving
Windsurfing
Golfing
Hiking

SPORTS & RECREATION

Prior to the arrival of Europeans, Hawaiians had developed a variety of sports and games and have always been enthusiastic sportsmen. Traditional sports and games are too numerous to detail here. The ones still popular today are surfing (which has spread to many parts of the world) and outrigger canoe racing, though they have been substantially altered from the way they were done in ancient times. Hawaiians also took readily to many of the sports introduced by various immigrants to these islands, and today the people of Hawai'i participate in a wide cross section of recreational and competitive events. Favored snorkeling and surfing areas are noted in the BEACHES section. Phone numbers and addresses of sports equipment rental companies are listed at the back of this book.

SNORKELING

Snorkeling provides easy access to the colorful underwater world. Snorkels, masks and fins are available from **Snorkel Bob's** in Lihu'e and Po'ipū, **Kaua'i Snorkel Rental** in Kapa'a, **Fathom Five Adventures** in Po'ipū, **Pedal & Paddle** in Hanalei, and at all the dive shops listed below. All operators of water tours provide snorkeling equipment as part of the package. Underwater cameras are available for rental from **Dive Kaua'i Scuba Center** in Kapa'a and **Pedal & Paddle** in Hanalei, among others, as well as on some of the escorted snorkel tours.

Good snorkeling areas are noted in the BEACHES section of this book.

SCUBA DIVING

Take a tank dive for an even deeper look at Kaua'i's undersea environment. Certified divers may rent equipment and go out on their own, or may arrange a chartered excursion. Those unfamiliar with local conditions are encouraged to take an escort, as this sport is potentially dangerous, even for trained divers. Introductory classes are available for those seeking certification.

Dives take place wherever conditions are best at the time; this generally means the north shore in summer and the south shore in winter, as this is the prevailing pattern of calm waters. Depths range from twenty to a hundred and fifty feet, with most areas falling into the middle of that spectrum. An excellent island-by-island guidebook is available which the local diving community considers the ultimate resource for diving Hawaii's waters, called *Hawaii Below: Favorites, Tips and Secrets of the Diving Pros* by Rod Canham. Serious divers may want to pick up a copy.

Though there is good shore diving along much of Kaua'i's coastline, most of the island's top dive spots are accessible only by boat. Some very good diving is found off the Polihale coast in the area known as **Mānā Crack.** Several interesting sites lie off the southwest coast. Near Kukui'ula Bay, a site with the popular name **General Store** is the location of a nineteenth-century shipwreck, and two caverns are home to a large variety of colorful tropical fishes.

Off Ka'ūlala Point, **Oasis Reef,** a solitary pinnacle surrounded by sand, attracts lots of fishes, octopi, lobsters and moray eels. Near Na-humā'alo Point, ledges and holes of the lava terraces at **Fishbowl** attract an excellent variety of fish which like to be hand-fed. Off Po'ipū, three large parallel lava tubes collectively known as **Sheraton Caverns** form one of Kaua'i's most popular dive spots. One shelters a lobster nursery; all are frequently visited by large turtles

sharks occasionally visit the area. The reef areas off Līhu'e Airport offer three good dive spots.

Near Nāwiliwili Bay, **Aquarium** has a good variety of both corals and fishes as well as several cannons from an eighteenth-century ship-wreck. An unusual formation called **Dragon's Head** is named for its appearance; many of its caverns contain rare black coral and large fish such as *ulua* (jack crevalle) and rays frequent the area. There are also lots of crustaceans under ledges and in holes.

Kaua'i's oldest boat harbor, **Ahukini Landing** (now unused) is popular for introductory dives and

Ideal dive spots ring Kaua'i's coastline.

and, occasionally, by whitetip reef sharks.

The reef off Brennecke's drops off sharply, creating **Brennecke's Drop,** a long ledge with many holes and overhangs where turtles frequently sleep. Some interesting coral types also grow here, and whitetip reef

has a good variety of fish as well as interesting coral formations such as the unusual plate coral. Off the cliffs of the Princeville coast, the awesome drop-off of **Do Drop In** has large formations of many types of coral, including trees of black coral, and abundant reef fishes. For experts only is the spectacular dive spot known as **Oceanarium** where tall pinnacles and sheer, deep drop-offs display excellent coral formations and attract large fish such as barracuda, rays and *ulua*.

The only one of the island's dozen top dive spots accessible from shore, **Cannon's Reef,** lies off the western end of Hā'ena Beach. Turtles are common in the area, and whitetip reef sharks can be found cruising the long ledge or sleeping in caverns formed by lava tubes. There are also good diving spots along the Nā Pali Coast. Because of high winter surf conditions, north shore sites are diveable only in summer.

Kaua'i's dive tour companies include **Fathom Five Adventures** (742-6991) in Po'ipū, **Dive Kaua'i** in Kapa'a (822-0452), **Ocean Odyssey** in Waipouli (245-8681), **Aquatic Adventures** in Kapa'a (822-1434), **Bubbles Below** in Kapa'a (822-3483) and **Bay Island Water Sports** at the Princeville Hotel (826-7509). All give instruction for certification to varying levels and some do night dives. **Aquatic Adventures, Dive Kaua'i, Fathom Five** and **Ocean Odyssey** also rent underwater cameras. Prescription masks, for those who need them, are available at **Dive Kaua'i, Bubbles Below, Fathom Five** and **Bay Island Water Sports.** Scuba lessons are also available from the beach service concessions at some of the large hotels.

SNUBA

Halfway between snorkeling and scuba diving, a new water activity has arisen called "Snuba". Divers are connected to an air tank mounted on a raft floating above them, and are able to breathe freely via a twenty foot air hose, unencumbered by a bulky, restrictive oxygen tank. Escorted by a certified dive master, these underwater tours are provided by **SNUBA Tours of Kaua'i** off of Lāwai Beach in Po'ipū. Rates run $49.00 per person. For more information, call 823-8912.

Snorkeling satisfies the most curious of visitors.

SURFING

Since these island-based people lived constantly within reach of the sea and its changing waves, it is not surprising that Polynesians invented the sport of surfing. While many other Polynesian groups enjoyed riding surf in their outrigger canoes, Hawaiians alone developed the art of riding boards specifically designed for play atop the rolling waves.

In modern times, this ancient sport has been refined and extended beyond anything its inventors ever imagined, and its popularity has spread around the globe. Professional surfers demonstrate their skill and daring while vying for six-figure purses. The manufacture of surfing equipment also developed as well as, in recent years, the new variant: windsurfing. The areas best suited to surfing and windsurfing are noted in the BEACHES section.

BOARD SURFING

This is the original. No one knows how long ago it developed, but Hawaiian petroglyphs dated to about the eighth or ninth century show people board surfing, and, as early as the fifteenth century, Hawaiians had so refined the sport that contests between champions were held for what even we would consider to be high stakes. Ancient Hawaiians gambled with unbridled enthusiasm at every opportunity, wagering their property, their wives, even their lives on the outcome of a single game.

Many famous surfing exploits were passed down through the voluminous oral history of these people. Their name for what we now call surfing was *he'enalu*, which can be loosely translated as 'wave sliding' but which, like everything else in the Hawaiian language, is rich with a range of subtlety and poetic nuance that says much more. The best surfing breaks were reserved for use by the ruling chiefs, and violators of this *kapu* could be punished by death.

Surfing, like all things Hawaiian, declined dramatically during the first century or so of European immigra-

tion to the islands, but surfing, both on boards and in canoes, began to be promoted again in Hawai'i early this century. Surfing's international fame began to spread with demonstrations in Atlantic City and Australia that were given by surfing champion and Olympic gold medal swimmer Duke Kahanamoku.

The original boards were eighteen-foot, hundred-and-fifty-pound monoliths, often made of koa wood. This began to change in the mid-1940s with the development of hollow boards and ones built of such lightweight materials as balsa and redwood, then fiberglass and synthetic foam. The evolution of surfboards has also seen a wide variety of lengths, widths and thickness, and these variations on the theme have been found to excel in varying conditions so that, today, top surfers keep collections of several boards from which to choose.

The activities desks at the major hotels are good resources for renting surfboards, as well as **Kauai Water Ski and Surf** in Kapa'a (822-3574), **Hanalei Surf Company** in Hanalei (826-9000) and **Progressive Expressions** in Po'ipū (742-6041). **Hanalei**

Surf Company also offers private surfing lessons, as does world champion surfer **Margo Oberg** (742-1750), who many regard as the best surfing instructor on Kaua'i. Margo's "classroom" is off the beach at Kiahuna Plantation Resort at Po'ipū Beach.

Body surfing

This is a cross between board surfing and swimming and stems from the same principle as board riding, except that the body replaces the board as the vehicle. The ancient Hawaiians called this activity *kaha nalu* or *pae* or *paepo'o*. There are two basic techniques for accomplishing this feat: keeping the body straight with the arms pinned against the sides while riding the shoulder of the wave just ahead of the breaking water, and the alternative of keeping one or both arms straight out in front for greater maneuverability. The former technique seems to work best in offshore breaks while the latter seems best in the large, shallow shorebreaks.

Most expert bodysurfers use both, sometimes while riding the same wave. Though purists decry it, virtually all bodysurfers also use fins to increase propulsion and enhance their ability to catch a wave.

Paipo boarding

The term *paipo* is a post-World War II corruption of the Hawaiian word *paepo'o*, and essentially is a 'bellyboard'. This type of wave-riding board is short and thin--three or four feet long and only a quarter to half an inch thick--either flat or with a slightly concave surface to fit the body. They are mostly home-made and primarily used by Hawaiians. Their use requires skill and they have been largely superseded in popularity by the now well-known 'Boogie (TM) board'.

Body boarding

The body board, developed from the *paipo* board described above, was invented in Hawai'i in the early 1970s by Tom Morey, and is made of flexible foam. The 'boards' are a couple of feet wide, about four feet long and around three inches thick, and, like their parent *paipo*, are ridden prone. The latest development along this line is a high performance body board (now termed 'turbo-board') that was invented by Russ Brown in 1983. Considered the Porsche of body boards, it is stiffer and faster than the standard model. These inexpensive water toys have become ubiquitous in Hawai'i, and are readily available for rental or sale all over the island.

Some of the places you can find them are: **Progressive Expressions** and **Fathom Five** in Po'ipū, and **Kaua'i Water Ski & Surf**, **Dive Kaua'i** and **Aquatic Adventures** in Kapa'a.

Sand sliding

This, too is an ancient pastime that has been given a modern tool. The original idea was to throw oneself onto the sand at the precise moment when a receding wave had left just a thin sheet of water on which the body would then slide. Precise timing was (and is) essential, as too early a leap results in a mere sinking to the sand and leaping too late results in an abrupt abrasive halt.

Bare-body sand sliding is seldom seen anymore, but *paipo* boards and the more recent body boards are also used in this fashion. Nowadays the hot trend is the 'skimboard', a short foam 'board' about three quarters of an inch thick that is thrown onto the receding wave then jumped upon.

Skilled standing riders have developed some fancy skateboard-like maneuvers on this type of board, and contests have been held on O'ahu. It can also be ridden as a 'bellyboard' in waves.

WINDSURFING

The most imaginative modern variation of the ancient sport of surfing was its hybridization with sailing, conceived in 1970 by Californian Hoyle Schweitzer and executed by his friend, Jim Drake. The popularity of this new sport spread like wildfire and a circuit of amateur and professional contests is already well established.

'Anini Beach is Kaua'i's best windsurfing spot because its waters are protected by Hawai'i's largest fringing reef and the prevailing

Surfing is not just a sport, but a way of life to some.

northeast tradewinds blow fairly steadily onshore. These conditions also make it one of the easiest places to learn.

Windsurfing specialist **'Anini Beach Windsurfing** (826-9463) offers professional instruction at all levels.

Lessons run $25 per hour, or you can rent your own board for $50 per day. **Hanalei Sailboards** (826-9000) also provides expert instruction, as does certified master instructor, **Celeste Harvel** of Hanalei (828-6838).

SAILING

Kaua'i's waters offer exquisite sailing, with the north shore in summer and the south shore year-round being ideal for this activity. Currently small sailboats are not available to rent on your own, so it is best to take one of the many charter boat or sight-seeing tours. Sunset sails and picnic/snorkel cruises abound, and you will find information and brochures available at any activities desk in hotels or condominiums throughout the island.

Capt. Andy's Sailing Adventures is a favorite with visitors, offering three types of excursions aboard their comfortable 55-foot catamaran: a five- to six-hour tour of the Nā Pali Coast with a buffet deli lunch and two snorkeling stops ($95.00 per person), a four-hour Po'ipū Picnic outing ($65.00 per person), and a two-hour sunset cruise with drinks and hors d'oeuvres ($40.00 per person). Call 822-7833 for reservations and current tour schedule.

KAYAKING

Now very popular in Hawai'i, this ancient Eskimo pastime translates well to the tropics. There are also canoe/kayak hybrids. **Island Adventure** in Līhu'e (245-9662) runs two-hour river adventures out of Nāwiliwili Harbor and, on a charter basis, runs trips along the north shore in summer and the south shore in winter, as well as overnight expeditions to other islands. **Pedal & Paddle** in Hanalei (826-9069) and

Kapa'a (822-2005) rents kayaks and canoes, as well as wave skis, a modern cross between a kayak and a surfboard. Kayaks can also be rented from **Outfitters Kaua'i** in Po'ipū (742-9667), **Kaua'i Water Ski & Surf** in Kapa'a (822-3574), **Kayak Kaua'i Outfitters** in Hanalei (826-9844), **Paradise River Rentals** at Kilohana Plantation (245-9580), and **Chris the Fun Lady** in Waipouli (822-7447).

CANOEING

Want to experience the island in a Hawaiian sailing canoe? **Hanalei Beach Boys** offers a scenic two-hour trip down the Hanalei River and into

Hanalei Bay. Call Hanalei Surf Company (826-9000) for reservations.

Kayaking to shore before a storm

WATER SKIING

The most popular place on the island for water skiing is the broad, smooth Wailua River. The veteran operator here is **Kaua'i Water Ski & Surf** (822-3574), who has been pulling skiers up and down the river for almost twenty years. Ski boat, driver and all the equipment are included in a package rate of $85 per hour. Instruction, if desired, is part of the package at no extra cost.

TENNIS

Almost every hotel and condominium complex on Kaua'i has tennis courts, some of which may also be used by non-residents, with permission. The Kaua'i County Department of Parks and Recreation (241-6660) has public courts throughout the island. There is no fee to use these courts, but reservations are necessary. Additionally, there are public courts which charge hourly rates at the **Princeville Tennis Center** (826-3620), **Kaua'i Lagoons Racquet Club** in Līhu'e (241-6000), and **Kiahuna Tennis Club** in Po'ipū (742-9533).

GOLFING

Kaua'i has several excellent golf courses. The **Princeville Resort's** (826-5004) **Prince Course** is ranked by *Golf Digest* as Hawai'i's No. 1 golf course. The Resort's **Makai Course** is ranked by *Golf Digest* in its "Top 50 Resort Courses", and both have been included in "America's 100 Great Golf Courses". These thirty-six holes of golf were designed by Robert Trent Jones, Jr., and represent what many consider the peak golfing experience here in Hawaii. **Kaua'i Lagoons Golf and Racquet Club** (241-6000) offers 36 challenging holes of golf, with its Jack Nicklaus-designed **Lagoons Course,** ranked in the top ten of "America's Most Playable Golf Courses" by *Golf Digest,* and the **Kiele Course,** named "America's Best New Resort Golf Course" by *Golf Digest* in 1989.

The **Kukuiolono Golf Course** (332-9151), formerly part of the McBryde Estate in Kalāheo, is set in exquisite gardens and offers spectacular ocean views. The fees are unbeatable at $5 per day! Electric golf carts rent for $6, and pull carts are $1 (per nine holes). No reservations are taken for this course, with tee times assigned on a first-come, first served basis.

The **Po'ipū Bay Resort Golf Course** (742-8711), adjacent to the Hyatt Regency Kaua'i in Kōloa, is another Robert Trent Jones Jr. design. Although not considered as challenging as some of Kaua'i's other courses, the views are spectacular.

The Kaua'i County Department of Parks and Recreation's **Wailua Golf Course** (241-6666) has eighteen holes and a driving range, as well as a restaurant and cocktail lounge.

HORSEBACK RIDING

There are lots of scenic trail rides on Kaua'i, both along the beaches and into the mountains. Excursions last from one to several hours; the longer ones include picnics. **Po'oku Stables** in Hanalei (826-6777) offers interesting explorations on the north shore and features a four-hour waterfall/picnic tour (9:00 and 11:00 a.m., Monday through Saturday).

South shore rides are available from **CJM Country Stables** in Po'ipū (742-6096), offering a selection of three picturesque rides; west-side rides in the Waimea area are available from **Garden Island Ranch** (338-0052), and include an intimate two-person outing through the scenic lower west rim of Waimea Canyon.

HUNTING

Kaua'i has a lot of wilderness land where hunting is permitted, the most common quarry being feral pigs and goats, which are prolific and can be hunted, with varying restrictions, on weekends and holidays year-round. Black-tailed deer can be taken during a limited period in early autumn. Pheasants,

state holidays only.

Maps of public hunting areas are available from the Division of Forestry and Wildlife (241-3433 on Kaua'i or 587-0166 on O'ahu). All hunting requires a valid State of Hawai'i Hunting License; non-resident hunting licenses cost $10.00 and may be purchased from licensed

A relaxing horseback ride under sunny Princeville skies

quail, francolin and doves can be hunted on weekends and state holidays only from November until the third week in January. Barred doves can also be taken on private land with the owner's permission during February and March and July through October, on weekends and

agents at sporting goods stores or from the Division of Conservation and Resources Enforcement (1151 Punchbowl Street, Rm. 330, Honolulu, 96813 - 587-0077). For the most recent hunting statistics state-wide, call the Hunting Seasons Hotline at (808) 587-0171 for a recorded message.

FISHING

Freshwater fishermen must obtain licenses, but permits are not needed for recreational ocean fishing. Non-resident licenses effective for thirty days cost $3.50 and may be obtained at any major sporting goods store or the Division of Conservation and Resources Enforcement office (241-3521, Kaua'i). The season is open year-round for most fish.

Kaua'i has many rivers and streams, but most are on private land and access can be problematic. Several kinds of bass, tilapia, and a few types of catfish were stocked decades ago into many of the island's reservoirs, which provide water for irrigation of sugarcane fields.

Shore fishing is popular at many places along the coast. Surf casting gear can be rented from **Yoshimura Store** in Kapa'a (822-4457), and the friendly staff can also give you seasonal information about what fish can be found where.

Deep sea fishing lures a lot of enthusiasts to Hawaiian waters to catch *mahimahi* (dolphin fish) and, if lucky, *a'u* (marlin). Kaua'i has a number of companies offering sport fishing charters. **Sport Fishing Kaua'i** in Kōloa (742-7013) offers trips of varying lengths, as does **Gent-Lee**

Fishing and Sightseeing Charters (245-7504), operating out of Nāwiliwili Harbor. **True Blue Charters** (246-6333) and **Sea Lure** (822-5963) are also out of Nāwiliwili Harbor, operating 30-foot boats and specializing in small group excursions.

Liko Kaua'i Cruises (338-0333) operates a Coast Guard certified 38-foot custom Radoncraft along the Nā Pali Coast. Although the boat's maximum capacity is thirty, they limit their passengers to twenty-four for additional comfort on this combination snorkeling/fishing/sight-seeing tour. **'Anini Fishing Charters** (828-1285) has a 30-foot Coast Guard approved boat, the **Sea Breeze IV,** and takes six to eight passengers out on half-, three-quarters- and full-day fishing excursions off the north shore.

Advance reservations should be made for these fishing trips, and most can be arranged on a share basis or as private charters. Aficionados know this is not an inexpensive pastime. Most operators keep at least some of the fish caught, and it is customary to tip the skipper and mate, especially if the catch is good.

HIKING

Kaua'i is a hiker's paradise. Most of the island remains in a natural state because so much of it is difficult to reach except on foot, and then only with considerable effort. The rewards are unparalleled views, tropical vegetation, streams, waterfalls, swimming holes, and, above all, exquisite isolation. There are long and short trails, difficult and easy trails, but it is important to

remember that to camp in a state campground you must obtain a state permit (Division of State Parks, 3060 Eiwa St., Rm. 306, Lihu'e, Hawai'i 96766 - 241-3444), a county permit for a county campground (Division of Parks and Recreation, 4193-A Hardy St., Bldg. #5, Lihu'e, Hawai'i 96766 - 241-6660). Permits are free of charge.

The **Sierra Club, Hawai'i Chapter** (1111 Bishop St., Ste. 511, Honolulu,

Hawai'i 96813 - 538-6616) will, for a small fee, send an information packet describing state trails and trip-planning information. The Sierra Club offers numerous day hikes throughout the islands and welcomes visitors to join them. The **Hawai'i Geographic Society** (49 S. Hotel Street, Ste. 218, Honolulu, Hawai'i 96813) offers books, maps and other publications and requests written inquiries from Hawai'i-bound hikers. The **Hawai'i State Department of Land and Natural Resources, Forestry and Wildlife Division** (1151 Punchbowl St., Rm. 325, Honolulu, Hawai'i 96813 - 587-0166) has free trail maps. Highly recommended is the inexpensive handbook, *Hiking Kaua'i,* by Robert Smith, which provides extensive personally validated information on all the island's hiking trails.

Kaua'i's most extensive network of trails crisscrosses the upland forests and chasms of Kōkee State Park, Waimea Canyon State Park and the Alaka'i Wilderness Preserve. Altogether, there are twenty-eight named trails totalling forty-five miles in length through this unspoiled environment, rich in native flora and fauna, some of which is found nowhere else. A map of these is available from Kōkee Lodge and in hiking books. For their own safety in the event of an emergency, hikers should sign out at Park Headquarters before setting out, and sign in again upon returning. There are numerous wilderness campsites in the area.

In the southeastern quadrant of the island, an inland trek (2.5 miles) to **Kilohana Crater** follows a cane haul road and leads to an abandoned house on the northeastern flank that was once a holiday retreat for pineapple plantation staff. The route passes working cane fields, providing a close-up view of plantation procedures; fruits, flowers and trees of interest ring the crater. The land belongs to Līhu'e Plantation and permission for this hike should be requested from their office at 2970 Kele Street (next to the Post Office), Līhu'e. Park at the base of the private road next to the Halenānahu Reservoir, about two and a half miles west of Puhi.

About three miles upstream from the ocean on the South Fork of the Wailua River, **Wailua Falls** plunge eighty feet to a pool below. This is a twin waterfall, but it is not for this reason that the river is called Wailua (two waters); the river itself has two main branches--the North and the South Forks--which merge about a mile from the sea. From the lookout point beside the falls, a steep trail descends the cliff just south of the guardrail. This trail (.5 mile) is strenuous at the best of times and after rain can be slippery and dangerous. Several short trails lead from the end of the road to the stream above the falls.

Behind Wailua, **Nounou Ridge,** known as **Sleeping Giant,** can be climbed from either side. The trail on the *mauka* side (2 miles) climbs 1250 feet, the shorter *makai* side trail (1.5 mile) climbs about 1000 feet; the two run together around half a mile from the shelter at the end. Another half mile of fairly scary walking and crawling across short, narrow ridges brings you to the giant's chin and his forehead. The *mauka* trail runs off Kāmala Road (581), which is up the hill behind Coco Palms Resort, off Kuamo'o Road (580); the *makai* trail is about a mile or so up Hale'ilio Road, which runs *mauka* off Kūhiō Highway (56) just north of Coco Palms. In both cases, the trailheads

Rocky shores mark the end of Polihale Beach.

are clearly marked. Following Kuamo'o Road (580) *mauka* for about two and a half miles past 'Ōpaeka'a Falls to the University of Hawai'i Experimental Station brings you to an unpaved road leading to the **Keahua Arboretum**. A pamphlet available from a box on the site guides a walk (.5 mile) around the Division of Forestry project, giving details of the plants to be seen there. Across the stream, a sign marks the trailhead for the **Kuilau Ridge Trail** (2 miles) which snakes upward, affording beautiful views and, along a twisting stretch between two picnic shelters, past several small waterfalls before joining the Moalepe Trail.

The **Moalepe Trail** begins at the junction of Waipouli Road and 'Olohena Road, which can be reached from Wailua via Kuamo'o Road (580), Kāmala Road (581) to 'Olohena Road, or from Kapa'a via 'Olohena Road (581) off Kūhiō Highway (56) just south of Kapa'a Beach Park. This trail (2.5 miles) at first crosses open country then enters forest and climbs into the Makaleha Mountain Range, being joined by the Kuilau Ridge Trail about half a mile before the lookout point at the end, which offers a spectacular panorama.

The most famous and most popular hike on Kaua'i is the **Kalalau Trail** (11 miles). That path through the wilderness begins at the end of Kūhiō Highway (56) on the island's north shore and crosses several small and a couple of larger valleys at the eastern end of the Nā Pali Coast, ending in the spectacular Kalalau Valley. Built centuries ago by the Hawaiians who once inhabited and cultivated these valleys, the trail still provides the only access to the hanging valleys and the only land access to Hanakāpī'ai and Kalalau, which also have beachheads. In

addition to the main trail, described in SIGHT-SEEING, about fifteen miles worth of side trails lead into the large valleys--**Hanakāpī'ai, Hanakoa** and **Kalalau**--which have pools and waterfalls galore to reward the efforts of determined hikers.

Though the first couple of miles of the main trail (to Hanakāpī'ai Beach) are not all that difficult, virtually all the hiking available after that is on the strenuous side. Any destination farther in than Hanakāpī'ai requires an overnight stay unless you are dropped off by boat at Kalalau Beach early in the morning and hike back out. If you choose this option, keep in mind that the view is very different depending on which way you're facing, so look back often. People exploring these wilderness areas should exercise extra caution as no emergency aid is nearby, and should also be aware that, though it is discouraged by the authorities, nudity is common and should not come as a shock to those hikers with more traditional views of propriety.

Backpacking and camping equipment (as well as advice) is available from **Pedal & Paddle** and **Kayak Kaua'i Outfitters** (742-7364) in Hanalei (826-9069), and **Outfitters Kaua'i** (742-9667) in Po'ipū. If you prefer to obtain your equipment in Honolulu, the **Bike Shop** at 1149 S. King Street in Honolulu (596-0588) and Windward City Shopping Center in Kaneohe (235-8722) has a good selection of camping gear and backpacks for sale or rent. See more about camping under the ACCOM-MODATION section.

There are also several interesting short treks that are better described as walks than hikes. Just past the Hanalei Bridge, straight ahead along the river bank as you come over the bridge heading upstream, a trail into the **Hanalei Valley** (1 mile) follows the river past taro fields, fruit trees, flowers and thickets of bamboo.

Just east of the Coast Guard station at the end of Pe'e Road in Po'ipū, a walk along the beach brings you to the site of some ancient petroglyphs, though these are at times covered with sand. Walking past the end of the road and toward the cliffs at Polihale State Park, you might be able to find the sites of Polihale Heiau and the sacred spring, and at Wailua, you can walk from Lydgate around the river mouth--passing more, similarly sand-shrouded petroglyphs--to the bridge and, crossing the bridge, up the other bank to reach Holoholokū Heiau.

KITE FLYING

Ancient Hawaiians enjoyed flying kites, made of *tapa* or finely woven sail matting, that were six or seven feet wide and up to fifteen feet long. Kaua'i's beaches are terrific and popular places for flying kites. If you didn't bring yours and want to join in the fun, stop into **Kaua'i Kite and Hobby** at Princeville Center (826-9144). You won't find an ancient Hawaiian model, but there are some fabulous modern creations around, mostly in brightly-colored nylon. If you prefer to rent a kite, **Paradise River Rentals** at Kilohana Plantation (Lihu'e area) offers rentals (245-9580).

Two kite stores in Honolulu, which offer a wide selection of sport kites as well as lessons, are **High Performance Kites** at Ala Moana Center (947-7097) and **Kite Fantasy** (922-5483) at Kaimana Beach, across from Kapi'olani Park (Diamond Head end of Waikiki).

FITNESS CENTERS & SPAS

Jogging, running, aerobics, and fully-equipped spas and gyms are popular on Kaua'i, as elsewhere.

The Kaua'i Athletic Club (245-5381), located in Lihu'e's Kukui Grove Center, has a full range of weights, Nautilus machines and other standard gym equipment, a swimming pool and Jacuzzi, racquetball courts, steam rooms, saunas and full locker facilities. A healthy deli offers low-fat fare, and their Body Shop sells a full line of active wear. The daily use fee is $12.00 per person and is all-inclusive, with a discounted rate available for Hawai'i residents. Walk-in traffic is fine, as no advance notice is necessary to use the club. Open daily, weekdays from 6:00 a.m. to 10:00 p.m., and weekends from 8:00 a.m. to 6:00 p.m. **Hamer Hed Fitness Center** (823-6334) is a new full-service fitness center, which opened in December of 1994, located beneath the Whale Tower at Kaua'i Village in Kapa'a. The facility features a pro shop, juice bar, aerobics room, free weights room, cardio-circuitry area, and men's and women's locker rooms equipped with dry cedar saunas. A variety of fitness classes are available. Hours are Monday through Friday 6:00 a.m. to 10:00 p.m., Saturdays 8:00 a.m. to 6:00 p.m., and Sundays from 8:00 a.m. to noon.

The Prince Health Club and Spa (826-5030) at the Prince Golf &

Hanakāpīʻai Beach and the Kalalau Trail continuing above it

Country Club in Princeville Resort is one of the best equipped spas in the country, with whirlpool, sauna, steam baths, state-of-the-art conditioning equipment, a 25-meter lap pool, aerobic exercise classes, and fitness training programs. The per-person use fee for Princeville Resort guests and visitors alike is $10.00 per day or $35.00 per week, and is all-inclusive. Relaxing massages and facials are available upon request for an additional charge. Open daily: weekdays from 7:00 a.m. to 8:00 p.m., Saturdays from 8:00 a.m. to 8:00 p.m., and Sundays from 8:00 a.m. to 6:00 p.m.

The **Anara Spa** (742-1234), located at the Hyatt Regency Kaua'i, 1571 Po'ipū Road in Kōloa, offers its spa services and facilities to Hyatt guests and non-guests alike. Open each day from 6:00 a.m. to 8:00 p.m., the daily facility fee is $10.00 per person for Hyatt guests and $18.00 for non-

guests. After 6:00 p.m., the rate drops to $5.00; use of the facility in conjunction with spa or salon service is $5.00. The spa facility fee includes: Turkish steam room, Finnish sauna, Swiss shower, open air lava rock shower garden, outdoor whirlpool and Jacuzzi, weight room, 25-yard lap pool, locker room, towels, amenities, spa wardrobe and unlimited fitness activities. Massage, skin care treatments, make-up lessons, body pampering, hair and nail care services and personal training sessions are all offered at an additional fee. Fitness classes, ranging from walks to step aerobics to high-energy aerobics are offered daily. No one under sixteen years of age is allowed in the spa. The casual **Spa Cafe**, located poolside, offers tasty low-fat cuisine geared toward the health-conscious, and is open from 11:00 a.m. to 2:00 p.m.

BICYCLING

For more information on renting bicycles and various bicycle tours, refer to "Bicycle" under the IN TRANSIT section of this book.

One of Kaua'i's ultimate bicycle adventures is offered by **Kauai Downhill** (245-1774, 800-234-1774), and is a four-hour, twelve-mile coast from Waimea Lookout to Kekaha, beginning with a sunrise continental breakfast at the rim of Waimea

Lookout. A maximum group of 13 riders is escorted by two professionally trained escorts. Sturdy mountain bikes are provided to riders, and are specially equipped with custom drum brakes. Windbreakers, helmets and gloves are supplied to all participants. The charge per adult is $60.00, and $50.00 for children (ages 12-14). Transportation round-trip from Līhu'e is included.

ENTERTAINMENT

Kaua'i's Nightlife
Lu'au
Hawaiian Music
Calendar of Events

ENTERTAINMENT & NIGHTLIFE

The idyllic rural environment of Kaua'i affords a limited supply of entertainment and nightlife, but more and more restaurant and hotel lounges are providing live music regularly, particularly during the after-dinner hours. A Polynesian show or *lu'au* is on almost every first-time visitor's agenda, and most seek out Hawaiian music, knowing they're not likely to find it anywhere else.

This section outlines the entertainment scene generally. Specifics change often, and details are available from free tourist publications (many list only advertisers) and from local newspapers, magazines and radio stations. Reliable sources include the weekly "Garden Island Calendar" in the Sunday edition of *The Garden Island* newspaper, and the semiannual *Kaua'i* magazine's "Upcoming Celebrations" section. This colorful magazine also presents interesting articles on local places, people and events.

POLYNESIAN SHOWS

On nearly every island in the Pacific, Polynesian or not, the 'Polynesian Show' has become virtually *de rigueur* tourist entertainment. These shows stage performances based on the traditional music, dance and costumes of Hawai'i, Tahiti, Samoa, New Zealand and, occasionally, Tonga and the Cook Islands; sometimes, primarily Melanesian Figi is also included.

Available on Kaua'i at all *lu'au* and dinner shows, these spectacles are glitzy, show-biz interpretations, and the Tahitian *tamure* almost invariably highlights the evening with its fast-paced hip-swiveling, grass skirts, tall headdresses and wildly beating drums. Another show-stopper is the Samoan fire dance or its close kin, the knife dance. Hawaiian hula is usually the *'auana*, or modern, variety, though some shows include a traditional *'olapa* or *kahiko* hula as well. The Maori (New Zealand) contributions are always a *poi* dance (*poi* in Maori is the white balls on string that the women manipulate so expertly in some of their dances), and the fierce *haka* where men challenge each other (and their audience) with spears and protruding tongues.

LU'AU

Undoubtedly, the *lu'au* is the most famous feast on visitors' entertainment menu. This highly-civilized Polynesian custom resembles the American Thanksgiving feast, except that the *lu'au* can be given at any time, for any reason. One good, traditional reason for a *lu'au* is to honor and entertain visitors, so your attendance at one is entirely appropriate. The feast is named after the taro tops (*lu'au*) that are always served at one. Cooked with coconut cream, they are delectably delicious and highly recommended. Other traditional fare on such occasions includes such dishes as *laulau*, small packages of fish, pork, chicken or beef, with taro tops, wrapped in *ti* or banana leaves and baked; *poi*, a thick, purplish-gray paste made from the cooked and pounded base of the taro plant (the staple starch food of the Hawaiians); *kalua* pig, traditionally cooked in an underground oven (*imu*); and *haupia*, a thick, creamy coconut pudding. The introduction of European and Asian foods to Hawai'i has added great variety to the culinary concoctions that are now traditional at a *lu'au*. There is so much to choose from that the *lu'au* can please the palate of almost everyone.

Though the focus of the feast is food, a *lu'au* includes a host of entertainments to feast the eye and ear as well. Music, dance, and usually a bit of comedy enhance the festive atmosphere and add to the fun. They are staged on a grand scale. Prices at the different venues are comparable, except at Tahiti Nui, which is a lot less expensive.

The closest thing you'll find to a private, family *lu'au* is the one held at **Tahiti Nui** in Hanalei (826-6277). Hosted by Tahitian matriarch Louise Marston, the evening's entertainment features hula of ancient Kaua'i by Halau o Hanalei and includes dances from Tahiti. The cost is a reasonable $38.00 for adults, $15.00 for children under twelve. *Lu'au* shows are held on Wednesdays and Fridays.

Smith's Tropical Paradise Garden Luau in Wailua (822-4654) includes an international pageant in the outdoor Lagoon Theater highlighting "The Golden People of Kaua'i". In addition to the Polynesian dances representing Tahiti, Hawai'i, New Zealand and Samoa, the revue includes dances from China, Japan and the Philippines, major contributors to Hawai'i's ethnic soup. This lively and interesting show is worth a peek, even if you have seen 'Polynesian shows' before. Trams run through the gardens at night, at a cost of $1.00 per person, and free shuttle service is available from the Wailua area. The *lu'au* and international pageant are held on Mondays, Wednesdays and Fridays from 5:00 to 9:00 p.m., and cost $43.75 for adults, and $26.00 for children.

The **Kaua'i Coconut Beach Resort's** *lu'au* show (822-3455, ext. 651) is the recipient of the Hawai'i Visitor's Bureau Kahili Award, the highest distinction of its "Keep it Hawai'i" program. *Lu'au* shows are held every night of the week but Friday, and begin with a Torchlighting Ceremony at 6:30 p.m. For those interested in watching the preparations of the *kalua* pig, the traditional Hawaiian Imu Ceremony begins at 10:45 a.m. This all-Hawaiian show is more authentic than some of the more "glitzy" Polynesian revues presented in the islands. The production's costumes and choreography were created by Kumu Hulu Kawaikapuokalani Hewitt, and the show explores the legends and folklore of Kaua'i. The cost is $47.00 for adults, and $28.00 for children ages six to twelve, with no charge for children five years old and younger.

Please note that all prices quoted are subject to change without notice. It is best to confirm all rates and event schedules when making reservations.

HULA

The hula is the heartbeat of Hawai'i. An integral part of the ritual life of the ancients, the old hula never died. New dances derived from it became popular entertainment for visiting sailors, who paid well to witness these alterations, but Hawaiians didn't fundamentally connect this new and lucrative enterprise with their sacred dance. Reviled by missionaries as 'obscene', the old dance was taken underground and taught in secret, while the new dance thrived in places where religious reformers held no sway. Thus, there developed two

Hula as an artform is taught to keiki (children) of all ages.

distinct classes of hula, the ancient and the modern.

Hula 'ōlapa, more recently known as *hula kahiko*, the old style, is performed to the accompaniment of chanting and percussion only. Traditionally, the dance was done to accompany the chant, which was of primary importance, and it was performed on most occasions by men. Though most hula groups today have a preponderance of women, the men's hula is every bit as beautiful, and is energetic with a virile grace that seems absent from the aggressive men's dances of other Polynesian cultures. Chanting, too, is an art that is experiencing a revival, along with the upsurge of interest in the Hawaiian language, which is always used in the chants.

The women's hula is softer than the men's, but still has strength and precision. Precision is a vital element of this hula style, and, while there is ample scope for the enactment of modern tales in the ancient mode, the rules are strict and strictly followed. There were, though, and still are distinctive hula styles, and Kaua'i's hula has special features (such as treadleboard percussion) that are primarily associated with that island.

It is interesting to note that the most famous symbol of the hula, indeed of Hawai'i--the grass skirt--is not Hawaiian at all. The grass skirt was introduced from Micronesia by laborers from the Gilbert Islands in the early nineteenth century. Hawaiians subsequently used native materials, such as *ti* leaves, in a similar fashion but they were always fresh and green out of respect for the gods, a strictly Hawaiian innovation.

Prior to European visitations, their garments had been made of bark cloth *(kapa)*. During the reign of King Kalakaua, when by royal decree the hula was again performed in public (earning him the nickname the "Merrie Monarch"), the European clothing of the time was worn in the dance, and hula from that era are still performed in costumes of the period.

Hula ku'i, a transitional form, which combines traditional hula movements with those of nineteenth-century European ballroom dance, arose at this time. Prior to this innovation, men and women seldom danced together; in most ancient hula performed today, they still do not.

Hula 'auana, the modern style, is much more flexible than its ancient forebear, just as modern ballet can be interpreted more freely than classical. Its costuming is limited only by the imagination and is keyed to the story being told. Modern hula is usually accompanied by both melody and lyrics as well as ukuleles, guitars and other instruments, and the songs may be in any language, though English and Hawaiian are most common.

There are many *halau* (hula schools), but their performances are not regularly scheduled. It's well worth scanning the local papers for *ho'olaule'a* or other community events (also see CALENDAR OF EVENTS) that feature hula, because what you see can be significantly different from what you may see in a Polynesian show, especially if you catch a good *kahiko*.

Free hula shows are presented at 4:30 p.m. on Monday, Wednesday, Friday and Saturday at the Coconut Marketplace, located between the Wailua River and Kapa'a. The world-famous *halau*, **Na Hula O Kaohiku-kapulani,** performs here under the leadership of Kumu Hula Kapu Kinimaka-Alquiza, a well-respected hula master. This *halau* has presented its expressive dances in cities throughout the mainland U. S. and Japan, receiving numerous accolades and awards of recognition, including one from Hawai'i's governor.

HAWAIIAN MUSIC

Though neither melody nor harmony had existed in Polynesian tradition prior to European contact, the people of the islands demonstrated remarkable natural affinity with and talent for both. They also adopted enthusiastically the stringed instruments these visitors introduced, and each Polynesian group has developed a distinctive musical style during the past century or two.

The guitar is probably the instrument most commonly used by contemporary Hawaiian musicians, but its baby brother, the ukulele, is most strongly identified with Hawai'i. 'Ukulele is, in fact, a Hawaiian word. It means 'leaping flea' and was first applied as a nickname to Edward Purvis, a popular nineteenth-century player of the instrument who jumped around while he strummed. Brought to Hawai'i by Portuguese laborers in 1879, the diminutive instrument was known to them as braquinho.

The other stringed instrument immutably linked with Hawai'i is the steel guitar, played horizontally with a metal slide. Last, but certainly not least, is the distinctively Hawaiian 'slack key' guitar, a tuning effect achieved by loosening the strings.

Today's island music has continued to evolve and is now less stereotypical and more grounded in true expression of the feelings of island life. Within it, naturally, are varieties--and insertions from the contemporary idiom--but the unique island flavor is discernible throughout.

Most of the large resort hotels have live Hawaiian music in their cocktail lounges and sometimes in restaurants during dinner hours. A stroll through any of them around the early evening is the best way to discover by just following your ears.

Hawaiian music is an integral part of island entertainment.

COCKTAIL LOUNGES & NIGHT SPOTS

When the sun goes down after a full day of sight-seeing and tan-cultivating, many people just want to relax and have a cocktail. To others, nightfall means jumping into high gear and dancing and schmoozing until the wee hours. Most lounges are quiet enough for audible conversation, however, most of the night-clubs fall into the 'too loud to talk' category.

The **Living Room** at the Princeville Hotel (826-9644) offers cocktails from 4:00 p.m. to midnight, with Hawaiian entertainment from 7:00 to 11:00 p.m. It's the perfect place to watch sunset over Hanalei. The **Lobby Lounge** at the Outrigger Kaua'i Beach Hotel (245-1955) has a full cocktail menu and live music nightly.

The Hyatt Regency Kaua'i's **Seaview Lounge** is located adjacent to the main lobby and live island entertainment is presented regularly from 5:30 to 9:30 p.m. The lounge offers a breathtaking view of Keoneloa Bay and features a "Vodkas of the World" bar. Also at the Hyatt, **Stevenson's Library,** is reminiscent of those dignified "gentlemen's clubs" of old. It's styled in the rich decor of the gentry set, with carved koa wood, game tables, pool tables, newspapers and books from around the world. Hours are 6:00 p.m. to 2:00 a.m. If you want to start your happy hour a bit earlier, **Captains** at the Hyatt is set in a gazebo by the pool and is open from noon to sunset, with nice views of the resort lagoons, pools and the ocean beyond. Call the Hyatt for more information - 742-1234.

Kaua'i Coconut Beach Resort's **Cook's Landing Lounge** (822-3455) overlooks beautiful gardens and a pool, and is open from 11:00 a.m., with soft, live music nightly, a mixture of Hawaiian and contemporary sounds.

The Happy Talk Lounge at the Hanalei Bay Resort (826-6522) offers one of the best views of the setting sun over Hanalei Bay and is one of the favorite establishments on the north shore.

If you want to turn up the volume, see and be seen, and perhaps dance the night away, **Gilligan's** disco at the Outrigger Kaua'i Beach Hotel (245-1955) near Lihu'e is the place to go. Loud, hard-hitting recorded rock music has the place jumping, and attracts a young crowd of twenty- and thirtysomethings. Hours are Thursday through Saturday 9:30 p.m. to 1:30 a.m. A comedy show is presented on Thursdays from 8:30 to 9:30 p.m. No cover charge except for the comedy show, which costs $12.00 per person.

Kūhiō's Nightclub at the Hyatt (742-6260) is a small, upscale club decorated in an elegant art deco style, and offers a variety of entertainment, depending on the night. Wednesdays feature Karaoke from 8:00 p.m. with free admittance and a small charge per song. Thursday is Comedy Night from 8:00 p.m. to midnight, with a $12.00 cover charge. Live music happens on Fridays, and costs $5.00 for Hyatt guests, $7.00 for non-guests. Saturday is "High Energy" night with recorded music from 8:00 p.m. to 1:00 a.m., with a $10.00 cover. This schedule is subject to change, so give them a call (742-1234) to confirm the current agenda. They do have a casual dress code, which calls for "a neat resort look".

Legends Nightclub (246-0491), a late night local hangout that often doesn't get rolling until past midnight. Located in Nāwiliwili, this hot spot on occasion features adult entertainment.

The **Jolly Roger** (822-3451) in Kapa'a offers mai tais at $1.95 each, and presents Karaoke nightly from 8:30 p.m. to 2:00 a.m.

A number of additional bars and cocktail lounges exist on the island, and anyone you ask will have a favorite spot to send you off to. Sometimes the most fun is exploring and stumbling onto a place all on your own, just as long as you don't over-imbibe and stumble on the way out. You've heard it before, but here's a bit of advice again. **Don't drive a car if you've been drinking alcoholic beverages.** Even with one's full wits about them, Kaua'i's roads crossing the island are very dark at night, and frequent downpours can make the pavement slippery and visibility poor. The thing to do if you plan on drinking is to appoint a designated non-drinking driver in your group, or leave the rental car behind and travel to and from by taxi. Sure, it may add to the cost of a fun evening, but you and your traveling companions can relax knowing you'll arrive back at your hotel safely.

THEATRE

The **Kaua'i Community Players** is a very active and talented amateur theatrical group which offers an almost continuous program of varying musical and dramatic plays throughout the year. Performances are generally held at the Parish Hall of the Congregational Church on Nāwiliwili Road in Līhu'e, opposite Kukui Grove Center, on Thursday, Friday and Saturday nights. Check the local newspapers or *Kaua'i* magazine for the current production.

CINEMA

Films currently showing at theaters on the U. S. mainland play at the local cinemas, which are located in Līhu'e at Kukui Grove Center (245-5055), and in Kapa'a at Coconut Plantation Marketplace (822-9391). Check the local newspaper for current program listings.

Kaua'i also hosts a scaled-down version of the **Hawai'i International Film Festival,** a major annual showing of films from Asian and Pacific nations sponsored each winter by the East-West Center in Honolulu and the State of Hawaii. Recently voted one of the world's top ten film festivals, it is the only free one. Watch newspaper listings in November for details.

ENTERTAINMENT

CALENDAR OF EVENTS

JANUARY

Brown Bags to Stardom--Amateur performers from around the island gather at the Kaua'i War Memorial Convention Center to take their turn in the spotlight.

FEBRUARY

Waimea Town Celebration--party with refreshments, food booths, games, rides, parade, entertainment, and 5K and 10K races. Waimea town.

MARCH

Prince Kūhiō Festival--pageantry, 10K race, songs and dances from the era of Prince Kūhiō. Canoe races and a royal ball.

APRIL

Polo season begins and runs throughout spring and summer at 'Anini Polo Field, Sundays.

Annual Easter Egg Hunt, Kukui Grove Shopping Center, Līhu'e.

Annual Businessman's Canoe Race, Wailua Bay, Hanamāulu, Kalapakī. Men and women representing local businesses compete in outrigger canoe races.

MAY

May Day (May 1) is Lei Day in Hawai'i--islandwide annual lei-making competition and exhibit, Kauai Museum, Līhu'e.

May Day by the Bay celebration, Hanalei--Crafts and ethnic food booths.

Taste of Hawaii--sample the best dishes by Hawaii's top chefs. Watch newspaper for announcement and schedule. Benefit sponsored by the Rotary Club of Kapa'a.

JUNE

Forest "Wonder Walks", Kōke'e Natural History Museum--Enjoy guided hikes on Kōke'e trails featuring stories of the history, plants and wildlife of the area. Repeated in July and August.

Annual King Kamehameha Celebration--June 12--Colorful floral floats, marching and mounted units. Street party follows in Līhu'e.

JULY

O'Bon Season July thru August. Colorful O'Bon dances and floating lantern ceremonies are held at various locations during Buddhist memorial season. Hongwanji missions of Kaua'i.

Na Hula O Kaohikukapulani-- Annual hula exhibition featuring the dances of Hawai'i and Polynesia. Līhu'e.

Kōloa Plantation Days--a week-long celebration in honor of the birth of sugar plantations in Hawai'i. Includes a historical parade, entertainment, crafts, games and the Miss Aloha Queen competition. Old Kōloa Town.

AUGUST

Trout Season opens, running through September. Trout are abundant in the streams at Kōke'e State Park. Call the division of Aquatic Services for information regarding dates and license requirements.

Na Holo Kai Sailing Canoe Race (90 miles) from Oahu to Kaua'i, starting from Pokai Bay.

SEPTEMBER

Kaua'i County Farm Fair-- exhibits, produce, flowers, 4-H livestock, rides, food and entertainment. Kaua'i War Memorial Convention Hall, Līhu'e.

Banana Poka Festival, Kōke'e Natural History Museum--annual forest education fair caps the summer with exhibits and fun for the whole family.

Kaua'i Mokihana Festival--pays tribute to the Hawaiian arts in a week-long celebration of events. Festivities are scheduled throughout the week at locations around the island.

OCTOBER

Aloha Festival--Hawaiian pageantry, canoe races, *hoolaulea* (street parties), parades and a variety of entertainment islandwide.

Kaua'i Loves You Triathlon--1.5K swim, 40K bike race and 10K run. Kalapakī Bay to Po'ipū.

NOVEMBER

Hawai'i International Film Festival--award-winning cross-cultural films from the Asia-Pacific area, shown free at several locations.

DECEMBER

Holiday craft fairs at locations throughout the island. Check newspaper for event locations and schedule.

SHOPPING

Centers
Aloha Wear
Art
Handcrafts

SHOPPING

M ost of Kaua'i's visitors go shopping for something during their island holiday. This categorized listing points out some of the more notable shops. Addresses and telephone numbers of these are listed at the back of this book as an appendix.

CENTERS

There are numerous shopping centers on Kaua'i; the big ones have a good cross section of shops and services, and many offer late night shopping. **Old Kōloa Town,** at the end of the famous Tunnel of Trees, is a delightful modern rendition of the old town center, the buildings having been renovated and the area revitalized. It's a pleasant setting for the wide variety of shops and boutiques that have congregated here and at night is lit up like a ship in port with strings of zillions of tiny white lights. Businesses include sports and tour companies as well as clothing, jewelry, art, flowers and photo needs, and several restaurants and snack shops. A jitney service shuttles shoppers around the town.

Kilohana in Puhi is part historic house museum and part shopping center, offering Hawaiian arts and crafts, clothing, jewelry and gifts as well as a popular restaurant (Gaylord's) and fine art galleries. Horse-drawn carriage rides around the grounds of this former plantation estate are narrated, giving the history of the family that owns it.

Poipū Shopping Village is a small center with a variety of shops offering t-shirts, fast foods, fine art, tour reservations, photo developing, gifts and sundries. **Waipouli Town Center** on Kūhiō Highway in Waipouli has a small range of shops and restaurants.

Ching Young Village Shopping Center in Hanalei has nineteen

businesses ranging from a travel agency to a beauty shop to a bicycle/ outdoor gear shop, to a bakery to an arcade to a video/music store to a supermarket to a pizza place. It has an outdoor stage where performances are held irregularly.

The Coconut Marketplace in Kapa'a is big, modern and beautiful, with more than seventy shops and boutiques, selling clothing, jewelry, island gifts, handcrafts and fine art, plus two cinemas and several restaurants, lounges and snack bars. It has an outdoor stage where a free Polynesian show is held Mondays, Wednesdays, Fridays and Saturdays at 4:30 p.m. Also in Kapa'a, **Kaua'i Village** offers more than forty interesting shops set in a unique plantation setting with plenty of parking, restaurants, and a Safeway market as the anchor store. **Kapa'a Shopping Center** has a Big Save supermarket, hardware store, bakery, laundry, Burger King, photo shop and a post office, among others.

Anchor Cove Shopping Center in Līhu'e has ten stores, and offers a free shuttle to and from Nāwiliwili Harbor. Here you can purchase t-shirts, fine art, photo finishing, lunch or dinner served oceanfront (J J's Broiler), ladies apparel, Hawaiian jewelry, convenience store items, and shoes. The center is open daily from 9:00 a.m. to 9:00 p.m. **Kukui Grove Center** in Līhu'e is a large, modern center, with three department stores: Liberty House, Sears and J C Penney, as well as K-Mart, Woolworth, Borders Books and Music, a drugstore, a supermarket, clothing boutiques, numerous eateries and small shops, plus a health club, a cinema and banking and professional services. This center also has an outdoor stage where performances are held.

Pacific Ocean Plaza provides more shops and restaurants, and is located at Nāwiliwili Harbor across from the Kaua'i Marriott. Rice Shopping Center in the heart of Līhu'e has a beauty shop, bowling alley, bakery/coffee shop, men's and women's clothing store and cocktail lounges.

Princeville Shopping Center has a large supermarket, bank and stores selling clothing, jewelry, photo supplies, flowers, kites, videos, ice cream and desserts as well as restaurants and a beauty salon.

Eleele Shopping Center in Eleele (Hanapēpē area) has fourteen businesses including a music store, bank, gift shop, hair salon, supermarket, travel agency, restaurant and post office.

ALOHA WEAR

Aloha shirts in bright flowery prints and *mu'umu'us* (long, loose dresses) put visitors in the lighthearted *aloha* spirit quicker than a mai-tai. People in Kaua'i really do wear these casual comfortable clothes, although couples with matching outfits are usually found only on stage.

The well-known Hilo Hattie's and the Happy Kauaian both have shops at the Coconut Marketplace with resort wear for the entire family; the latter also has locations at the Kaua'i Coconut Beach Resort, the Wailua Marina and a warehouse in Lāwai. The Kapaia Stitchery in Kapaia, at the edge of Līhu'e, carries island fashions for men and women, as does Remember Kaua'i at the Outrigger Kaua'i Beach. The large department stores, Liberty House, J C Penney and Sears, also have a selection of *aloha* attire.

DEPARTMENT STORES

Hawaii's homegrown department stores are Liberty House (Kukui Grove Center, Coconut Marketplace) and McInerny's (Hyatt Regency), and they carry the latest fashions in an atmosphere comparable to that of the U. S. mainland stores. J C Penney and Sears, both located at the Kukui Grove Center, differ little from their mainland branches, except they have *aloha* wear and Hawaiian souvenir departments.

T-SHIRTS

Everyone wears t-shirts, and their popularity never seems to fade. The classic success story and the undisputed king of trendy tees in Hawai'i is Crazy Shirts, located in Anchor Cove Shopping Center, Po'ipū Shopping Village, Old Kōloa Town and Kaua'i Village. A large selection of designs is available; their hallmark design is the delightful device of depicting on the back of the shirt a rear view of whatever is on the front.

There are several other t-shirt shops around, such as **Hawaiian T-Shirt & Hat Co., Poi Pounder Shirts, SanDudes of Kaua'i** and **Tropical Shirts.** But you can also find good quality t-shirts in clothing stores. If you're traveling to the north shore, check out t-shirts in gift shops along the road; they usually have interesting designs, but usually in small quantity.

SWIMWEAR

Kaua'i's swimwear specialists are **Swim Inn** in Old Kōloa Town, **Overboard** near Kiahuna Plantation, and **McInerny Waterware** in Po'ipū, as well as the three major department stores and many resort boutiques.

FABRIC

Those who prefer to craft their own tropical fashions when they get back home can find printed fabrics in shops such as **The Kapaia Stitchery** in Kapaia near Līhu'e, **Plantation Stitchery** at Coconut Marketplace, **Vicky's Fabric Shop** in Kapa'a and **Singer Hawai'i** in Kukui Grove Center.

LEATHER GOODS

Lee Sands in Lāwa'i on the corner of Kaumuali'i Highway (50) and Kōloa Road, has a wide range of accessories (including some jewelry) made from an astonishing array of exotic skins including eelskin, sharkskin, sea snake, salmon, and lizard.

JEWELRY

In Hawai'i, leis of tiny shells from Ni'ihau have long been treasured heirlooms. On Kaua'i, almost all jewelry and gift stores carry necklaces *(lei)*, bracelets *(kupe'e)* and earrings of Ni'ihau shells, the only shell classified as a gem and insurable. Difficult to see in their natural environment, these tiny, varicolored shells are found only on the small island of Ni'ihau and on the southwest coast of Kaua'i. Multiple strands fetch very high prices. The smaller *kahelelani* shells are the most expensive.

Kaua'i also has some fine jewelers making custom creations--such as **Jim Saylor Jewelers** and **The Goldsmith's Gallery,** both in Kapa'a. Fine shell, jade and other jewelry is available at **Kong Lung Co.** in Kīlauea. **Kaua'i Gold** in Coconut Marketplace has a nice selection of Ni'ihau shell leis and 14-carat gold jewelry.

Many jewelers, including **Prestige Jewelers** (Kukui Grove Center),

Robert's (Hanapēpē and Līhu'e) and **Capricorn Fine Gems** (Kaua'i Village) feature Hawaiian 'heirloom' jewelry--heavy bracelets and rings in gold with names enameled in black Victorian-style lettering. These are sometimes offered as transliterations into Hawaiian. You might like knowing what the word that sounds like your name actually means; check the *Hawaiian Dictionary*, by Mary Kawena Pukui and Samuel H. Elbert, or the book *Hawaiian Names*, by Eileen Root.

SCRIMSHAW

The whaling ships that sailed Hawai'i's waters and docked at her ports in the 1800s introduced the craft of scrimshaw carving to the islands. The intricate carving and etching techniques were passed down through the generations and scrimshaw pieces are quite valued today. Fossilized ivory and bone, as well as non-fossilized walrus tusks are shipped to Hawai'i from Alaska, carved with special tools and then etched in black, depicting sailing ships, whaling scenes and other artistic renderings, and fashioned into a variety of art objects and gift items. For environmental reasons, elephant ivory and whale bone are no longer used in scrimshaw. Eskimos are, however, legally allowed to hunt walrus for use in "Native American" artwork; even though they are not the actual artisans for Hawai'i's scrimshaw, they make some minuscule scratches on the tusks prior to shipping to meet government regulations.

Although the island of Maui offers the widest selection of scrimshaw, a few stores on Kaua'i do carry it. **Ye Olde Ship Store** in Coconut Marketplace is the largest scrimshaw dealer on the island, specializing in rare antique fossilized ivory.

Other dealers are **Kilohana Galleries** (Kilohana Plantation), **Shar's Scrimshaw** in Kapa'a, and **Ship Store Galleries** (Po'ipū Shopping Village and Coconut Marketplace).

ART

Kaua'i's tranquil tropical environment attracts artists of every ilk. One of the island's outstanding artists is **Laka Morton,** whose brooding portraits of Hawaiians have dramatic appeal. Hawaiian seascape master, **Roy Tabora,** paints as though he has light in his brush. Himself a resident of O'ahu, Tabora's sole agent in Kaua'i is **Kahn Galleries,** with locations in Coconut Marketplace, Kilohana Plantation, Hanalei and Anchor Cove Shopping Center at Līhu'e. This gallery also features a few other select artists, such as Jan Parker and George Sumner, as well as koa, sculpture, glass and jewelry.

One of America's leading environmental marine artists (famous for his "whaling" walls), **Wyland,** has thirteen galleries in the state, three of which are on Kaua'i and located at Kaua'i Village, Anchor Cove, and Po'ipū Shopping Village. **The Ship Store Gallery** in Coconut Marketplace and Po'ipū Shopping Center specializes in nautical art and antiques.

At Kilohana, **Kilohana Galleries** sells paintings, prints, ceramics and gifts. **Artists Gallery of Kaua'i** in

Hanalei's Ching Young Village and **Island Images** in Coconut Marketplace offer a similar range of creations by local artists.

Gallery Hanalei on the north shore specializes in exotic and contemporary Hawaiian artwork. **The James Hoyle Gallery** in Hanapēpē sells the pink and purple land- and seascapes of local painter James Hoyle. **Kashuba Fine Arts & Gold** in Lihu'e's Anchor Cove Shopping Center has a fine art collection and also sells original gold jewelry designs set with exotic gemstones.

HANDCRAFTS

Hawaiians traditionally woven and plaited the leaves of *hala*, or pandanus *(lauhala)* into all manner of useful items including floor mats and baskets; today the range has been expanded to include handbags, lamp shades, placemats and much more. Similar items are made in *tapa* (bark cloth), but this is not the traditional Hawaiian *kapa*, as the art of making the fine felt-like material the Hawaiians produced (the finest in all Polynesia) was lost generations ago. The *tapa* you buy here is, however, authentic; it is produced by hand using the ancient methods in Sāmoa, Tonga and Fiji.

Another traditional craft still very much alive and thriving is the making of permanent leis. These were and are made from feathers, seeds and shells. Ni'ihau shell leis now command hefty prices (see Jewelry above), but attractive strands of other local shells are quite reasonably priced. Feather leis are a bit more expensive, but require much more time and care in the making as well as more material.

Feather neck and head leis were traditionally worn by the *ali'i*, as were *lei niho palaoa*, hook-shaped pendants, originally made of whale ivory. Later made of wood or stone--or of walrus tusk or beef bone brought by merchant sailors--these hook-shaped pendants became so popular that virtually everyone wore them.

Woodcarving, too, has expanded far beyond its traditional application in creating *akua ki'i*, images representing gods. Indigenous woods such as koa, milo and monkeypod are carved into decorative bowls and utensils. You can also buy modern renditions of ancient gods, as well as more mundane figures such as fish and pineapples.

Most of these crafts can be found at gift stores all over Kaua'i. One such store, **The Country Store** at Kilohana Plantation, features an array of Kaua'i-made collectibles. Custom koa frames can be found at **Kaua'i Images** (Kapa'a), **Kaua'i Frame** (Hanamāulu), **Pictures Plus** (Kukui Grove Center), **8 Bells** (Kalāheo) and **Kaua'i Collectibles** (Kapa'a).

ANTIQUES

Treasures of Kuan Yin in Kapa'a features Asian artwork and collectibles. **Kaua'i Fine Arts** in Kōloa and Hanapēpē offer a selection of antique maps and prints. **Collectibles & Fine Junque** (Waimea) is self-explanatory.

FRUIT, FLOWERS and FOLIAGE

Cuttings and seeds of tropical plants provide a living reminder of a colorful Hawaiian holiday, and fresh fruits or flower leis make delightful gifts for presenting to friends back home. Shipping is easily arranged; many vendors will handle it for you. Some fruits and flowers are subject to quarantine regulations imposed by the U.S. Department of Agriculture and are prohibited entry into mainland states.

Pineapples are no problem (though few are grown on Kaua'i), but professional packing is preferable to ensure they arrive undamaged. The only papayas allowed are those treated, passed and sealed by agricultural inspectors. Only the frozen flesh of mangoes is allowed; the seeds are forbidden unless they are split open and inspected.

Guavas and passion fruit *(liliko'i)* are not allowed at all. Coconuts are fine and fun. Don't bother packing them; just buy them (or pick them up off the ground in an area where the trees remain untrimmed) still in the outer husk. This is excellent natural packing and has served to float coconuts for thousands of miles across open oceans to be dashed by waves, unharmed, upon foreign shores. Not only that, they survive shipment via the U. S. Postal Service. Just write the address on the coconut itself--unwrapped--and paste on the necessary postage stamps. The post office actually accepts these unorthodox parcels. **The Nutcracker Sweet** (822-4811) ships fresh fruit to the mainland; **Kaua'i Fruit & Flower Co.** (245-1814) will package pineapples and papayas for on-island delivery or shipping.

Be cautious when buying leis to take home. Flowers such as roses, *maunaloa* and jade, berries such as mock orange and *mokihana*, and leaves such as *hala* and *kikuyu* are prohibited; leis containing them will be confiscated. Many flower shops offer shipping service to the mainland. **Flowers Forever** (245-4717 and 826-7420), **Da Kine Floral Designs** in the Hyatt Regency (742-6247), **A Romantic Rose** (822-4781) and others offer this service.

For specific inquiries and further details, you may telephone the Kaua'i office of the State of Hawai'i Department of Agriculture at 241-3414 and ask for mainland export information. If you're leaving the country, you can take whatever you like, but there's no guarantee of its passing quarantine inspection in your country of arrival.

SOUVENIRS

Reasonably priced souvenirs and gift items can be found at **Longs Drug Store, K-Mart** and **Woolworth** in Kukui Grove Center. Another good, inexpensive place is **Village Variety** at Ching Young Village. **Waipouli Variety** located in Kapa'a and **Discount Variety** in Po'ipū and **Foodland** supermarkets also have souvenir sections.

More upbeat gifts and local craft items are found at many shops located in every hotel and shopping center on the island, as well as in a few out-of-the-way places.

SHELLS

Tropical shells are a popular souvenir item for visitors, but there are few to be found on the Island's accessible beaches. Numerous shops carry a wide variety of shells and an incredible potpourri of useful and decorative things made from shells. You may want to browse through **Shells International** and **Kaua'i Gold** (for Ni'ihau shell leis) at the Coconut Marketplace in Kapa'a.

Ni'ihau shell leis, made from hundreds of little white puka shells, are worn by Hawaii's women as a highly prized jewelry item and often passed down as family heirloom.

Beautiful Ni'ihau shell leis

BOOKS

At the back of this guide, we have listed books we recommend for more detailed information on Hawai'i. Most of these are easy to find in our local bookstores, but may be not so easy to find at home. Books are one of the surest ways to take a permanent remembrance of Hawai'i home with you. The huge mainland chain, **Waldenbooks,** has three shops on the island: Kukui Grove Center, Coconut Marketplace and Kaua'i Village. Their extensive Hawaiiana collection is overseen by knowledgeable, friendly staff. **Borders Books and Music** is Kaua'i's newest and largest bookstore, located next to K-Mart at Kukui Grove Center.

Kauaiana in particular is the natural specialty of the shop at the **Kaua'i Museum** in Līhu'e, which also carries a delightful range of gift items related to the museum's areas of interest. **Hanapēpē Bookstore/ Tropical Scents,** located in downtown Hanapēpē also carries Hawaiiana books as well as tropical potpourri, and has an espresso bar (The Espresso Bar). Hours are Wednesday through Sunday 8 a.m. to 3:00 p.m. Dinner is served Thursday, Friday and Saturday nights in The Espresso Bar.

CASSETTE TAPES and C.D's

For a wide selection of music, try **Borders Books and Music** in Kukui Grove Center or **Jack Wada Electronics** in Līhu'e. Another place to buy music is **Gem** in Līhu'e Shopping Center, at the junction of Kūhiō (56) and Kaumuali'i (50) Highways, offering a good selection of Hawaiian music. There's also **Ruby Tuesday** in Kapa'a or the **Hanapēpē Bookstore** in Hanapēpē, which has a nice offering of Hawaiian tapes and C.D.'s. The music of Kaua'i's most famous pop singer to date, Glenn Madeiros, is available at most of the above-mentioned stores.

GROCERIES

Those visitors with kitchen facilities may not choose to eat out for every meal. Local supermarkets carry most of the standard items that you're used to, and a lot more, including large sections of Oriental food items. Some visitors find a tour of the large grocery stores an amazing experience, especially in the produce department where you may see a number of things you don't recognize.

The large supermarket chains on Kaua'i are **Big Save**, with six locations around the island, **Foodland** in Princeville and Waipouli, **Safeway** in Kaua'i Village (Kapa'a), and **Star Market** in Kukui Grove Center. A delightful vestige of a bygone era is a genuine old general store, **Wainiha General Store,** on the north shore.

Favorite local snack foods found in most stores are: Waimea taro chips, Kaua'i Kookies, and an array of Yick Lung 'crack seed' (Oriental dried, salted fruit), as well as the delectable macadamia nut, available in a number of tasty concoctions such as chocolate- and honey-coated candies, fudge, cookies, rich cream pies, and ice cream.

CLOTHING STORES

Kaua'i has numerous specialty boutiques in virtually every town, which you'll have a good time exploring. Space restraints make it impossible to list them all, but here are a few worthwhile notables.

If you travel through Kilauea, stop in at the **Kong Lung Co.** store. In the late 1880s, the original Kong Lung Company was a Chinese plantation store operated by the Lung family. The plantation closed in 1969 and, with the rise in tourism, visitors began taking the side trip to Kilauea Lighthouse and Kong Lung once again began to flourish. In 1992, the store entered its second hundred years, and was purchased by north shore resident Patty Ewing. Newly refurbished after Hurricane Iniki and reopened for business in October of 1993, the store still retains the charm of its historic past. Its use of the spacious interior is both innovative and stylish, making you want to take your time ambling from room to room. The store offers an eclectic array of ladies' and men's casual clothes and accessories, stationery items and one-of-a-kind gifts and furniture.

Tropical Tantrum has been in operation since 1986, with three stores on the island (on the main highway in Kapa'a, in Hanalei Center, and their factory store in Kapa'a). Their casual line of clothes is designed locally and hand-painted or batiked, using every color in the rainbow. If you're looking for the perfect island-wear for Hawai'i's climate, this is a good shopping choice, featuring clothes for men, women and children, as well as a wide range of accessory items. Tropical Tantrum owners Lorre Johns and Parker Price opened a new store in 1994 called **Bamboo Silks,** near Tropical Tantrum in Hanalei (across from Ching Young Village), featuring exclusive hand-painted and batiked silks. Their merchandise features dresses, pants and skirt sets, and men's shirts, as well as accessories.

CONVENIENCE STORES

Menehune Food Marts are located at Kīlauea, Lāwai and Kalāheo; **7-Elevens** are found on Kūhiō Highway at Līhu'e and Hanamāulu. **ABC Discount Stores** are situated at Kaua'i Village, Anchor Cove Shopping Center, and Kapa'a (this location has a gas station). Also in Kapa'a is **Pono Market**. The **Happy Kauaian** convenience stores are located at Coconut Marketplace, Wailua Marina, and in the Kaua'i Coconut Beach Resort.

HEALTH FOOD STORES

Papaya's Garden Cafe and Market in Kaua'i Village (Kapa'a) is definitely worth a visit, especially if you're hungry, as it has a wonderful deli/cafe (see RESTAURANTS) and open-air tables in a pretty setting. The store has a very good selection of organic produce, natural body care products and cosmetics, as well as vitamins and supplements. The north shore's health food emporium is **Hanalei Health & Natural Foods** in Ching Young Village. Check out their delicious assortment of takeout food--healthy sandwiches and deli fare--prepared daily using fresh organic produce. In Kīlauea you'll find **Hale O'Health**, one of two stores on the island. On the east shore, it's **Ambrose's Kapuna Natural Foods** in Waipouli, **Hale O'Health** in Rice Shopping Center (Līhu'e) and **General Nutrition Center** in Kukui Grove Center, also in Līhu'e. A popular health-food item available in many stores around the island is Anahola Granola, made locally.

DRUGSTORES

The largest drugstore on Kaua'i is **Longs** at Kukui Grove Center. **Longs** is the type of drugstore that sells everything under the sun. **HPI Pharmacy** in Līhu'e and Waimea, **Shoreview Pharmacy** in Kapa'a, **North Shore Pharmacy** in Kīlauea, **Southshore Pharmacy** in Kōloa, **Menehune Pharmacy** in Waimea and **Westside Pharmacy** in Hanapēpē offer the standard drugstore services on a smaller scale.

DINING

The Best Restaurants in Kaua'i
Fast Foods
Ice Cream and Frozen Yogurt
Shave Ice
Espresso Bars
Bakeries

FINE and FUN DINING

Kaua'i offers a surprisingly large selection of diverse dining experiences, and even a few world-class restaurants. From haute cuisine to ice cream the Garden Island has plenty to offer, and you can pick a venue to suit almost any mood.

THE BEST RESTAURANTS ON KAUA'I

A selection of choice dining establishments, from inexpensive to expensive, from simple fare to gourmet cuisine, is listed here, arranged by area of the island. A complete list is included as an appendix at the back of this book. Fast food restaurants are listed at the end of this section.

The following symbols will assist you in choosing a restaurant to suit your requirements, taste and budget.

Price ranges indicated are per person and do not include drinks. Many of the restaurants on the island accept major credit cards.

B	Breakfast	$$$$	$40 +
L	Lunch	$$$	$30-$40
D	Dinner		
R	Reservations suggested	$$	$15-$30
E	Entertainment	$	$10-$15
W	Wheelchair access	No $	Less than $10

The following criteria were used in evaluating the quality of the restaurants listed in this section:
- taste, texture and presentation of food
- attentiveness and demeanor of service staff
- price in relation to food
- appropriateness of menu selections
- building and setting
- ambiance and decor

Dining in a waterfront setting enhances the tropical experience.

DINING

East Shore Area Restaurants

A Pacific Cafe $$ D, R 822-0013

Chef Jean-Marie Josselin's casual gourmet restaurant offers some of the best food you'll find in Hawai'i. European and Pacific Rim cuisine is featured on the *a la carte* menu, which changes daily. A variety of fresh local ingredients is used in each culinary delight, with fresh fish entrees the highlight of the menu. Their award-winning signature dish is wok-charred mahimahi and is superb. Portions are generous and filling, and the warm, freshly baked rolls served with the meal are delicious. Although the restaurant's shopping center location doesn't offer a view, and the place on busy evenings can be a bit on the noisy side, these features are more than made up for in the stylish decor, excellent European-quality service provided by energetic wait help, artistic food presentation and delectable cuisine. Reservations are strongly suggested, as the restaurant has become quite popular since its opening in 1990. *4-831 Kūhiō Hwy. (Kaua'i Village), Kapa'a*

Barbecue Inn B/L/D, R 245-2921

If you're looking for value and downright good food, this unpretentious eatery is highly recommended by local residents, offering a wide variety of beef, seafood and poultry entrees, served in generous portions. Delicious homemade bread and lavosh. Something on the menu for everyone. No credit cards accepted; closed Sundays. *2982 Kress Street, Līhu'e*

Bull Shed $/$$ D 822-3791

This is a favorite (since 1973) with both visitors and residents, specializing in seafood, fresh local fish, prime rib, Midwest beef, chicken, and rack of lamb. Entree portions are large, so come with a big appetite. Children's portions are available. Reservations only accepted for parties of six or larger, so anticipate a wait or get there early (they open at 5:30 p.m.). Dining is oceanfront, with waves sometimes splashing against the glass of the seaside windows. *796 Kūhiō Hwy., Waipouli (across from McDonalds, and just north of Coconut Marketplace, makai side)*

Cafe Portofino $$ L/D, R 245-2121

This cafe offers excellent authentic Italian food, good prices, attentive and friendly service, all in a bright, attractive setting. Entrees include a variety of fresh pasta, chicken, veal and beef dishes. Additional seating is available, weather permitting, on a pleasant open-air lanai, offering a partial view of Kalapaki Bay. Candlelit tables are set with crisp linen and spotless crystal. You won't be disappointed in this gem. Lunch served 11:00 a.m. to 2:00 p.m. Monday through Friday; dinner served nightly from 5:00 to 9:30 p.m. Reservations suggested. *3501 Rice St. (Pacific Ocean Plaza, across from Anchor Cove Shopping Center), Nāwiliwili*

DINING

105

Dragon Inn Chinese Restaurant $/$$ L/D, R   822-3788

Eat in or take out; if you like good Chinese food, this is the place. Both the food and service are excellent; the restaurant is clean, with simple decor. Generous portions served, and the prices are quite reasonable. *4-901 Kūhiō Hwy. (mauka side), Waipouli Plaza, second floor*

Flying Lobster/Voyage Room $-B/L,$$-D   B/L/D, R, W   822-3455

Called the Voyage Room during breakfast and lunch, and the Flying Lobster at dinner, this spacious open-air restaurant, at the Kaua'i Coconut Beach Resort in Kapa'a, offers reasonably priced fare, good food presentation and attentive service. Decorated with authentic artifacts and artworks, this eatery overlooks the hotel garden, with nice ocean views. They offer a special "Plantation Breakfast Buffet" with just about everything you'd want to eat in the morning. Or, you can order breakfast off the menu, if preferred. Lunch is either an extensive lunch buffet offering a trio of entrees and all the fixin's, or you can order from the menu; typical luncheon fare includes burgers, sandwiches and fresh salads. Dinner, as the name "Flying Lobster" implies, features slipper and spiny lobster, as well as a large assortment of entrees (steak, prime rib, fish, chicken, etc.) which change weekly. *Kaua'i Coconut Beach Resort, Kapa'a*

Gaylord's Restaurant $-L, $$/$$$-D   L/D, R   245-9593

Situated on the expansive and picturesque Kilohana Plantation, this 19th century estate is a romantic site for lunch or dinner. Tables are set around covered verandas, providing a delightful open-air setting. The continental menu includes seafood, meats and poultry, excellent desserts, and a good wine list. Sunday brunch served 9:30 a.m. to 3:00 p.m. Limousine and van service available for small groups. *Kilohana Plantation Estate, Kaumuali'i Hwy. (50), one mile southwest of Līhu'e.*

Hamura Saimin Stand   L   245-3271

Don't judge this place by its, well, "rustic" exterior; what's lost on decor is recovered in the food, touted as the best saimin on the island. Super-cheap prices for superb soup and saimin. Cash only; take-out orders. Pick up a shave ice on your way out, for an extra treat. *2956 Kress Street, Līhu'e*

Hanama'ulu Restaurant & Tea House $/$$ L/D, R   245-2511

A peaceful Japanese garden setting provides a relaxing ambiance for this unique restaurant, which specializes in Japanese and Chinese cuisine. Guests can enjoy their meal seated on mats at low tables next to a lovely koi pond, or in the teahouse, main dining room, *tepan yaki* room or at Ara's sushi bar. Private tea rooms may be reserved several days in advance. Food and service are excellent. Take-out orders also available. Reservations recommended. Closed Mondays. *On highway 56 in Hanamā'ulu, near Līhu'e*

JJ's Broiler $/$$ L/D, R 246-4422

Featuring casual oceanfront dining overlooking Kalapakī Bay, this was Kaua'i's original steak house, in business since 1968. Steak is their specialty, especially their Slavonic steak, a broiled tenderloin thinly sliced and dipped in a butter, wine and garlic sauce. The lunch menu offers salads, burgers, sandwiches, fresh fish, and teriyaki chicken, and also includes several vegetarian choices. Dinner features corn-fed premium beef, fresh fish, chicken, scallops, shrimp, and lobster tail. A popular beach park sits between the restaurant and the bay, and if crowded can detract somewhat from the picturesque view. Cocktail lounge downstairs with tables outside. Lunch is served from 11:00 a.m. to 5:00 p.m.; dinner is served from 5:00 to 10:00 p.m. *Anchor Cove Shopping Center, Nāwiliwili*

Jacaranda Terrace $-B/L, $$/$$$-D B/L/D, R,E,W 245-1955

A lovely, airy dining room overlooking the pool at the Outrigger Kaua'i Beach, this casual and relaxing restaurant has a beautiful garden/ocean view. Serves international and island favorites, with very good breakfast, lunch and dinner buffets. Fridays from 6:00 to 9:30 p.m., they offer an extensive seafood buffet, which includes lobster tail, steamed crab legs, pasta dishes, fish, roast baron of beef, seafood and vegetable tempura, salads, soups and appetizers. In short, you won't go away hungry! Entertainment nightly from 7:00 p.m., except on Wednesdays. *Outrigger Kaua'i Beach, Līhu'e*

Jolly Roger $ and less B/L/D 822-3451

For those on a budget, this is an inexpensive choice for any meal, and a favorite local breakfast spot. The food is satisfying and it's a good place to take the kids. The cocktail lounge features Karaoke from 8:30 p.m. to 2:00 a.m. nightly, offering $1.95 mai tais. Open daily. *Located just behind Coconut Marketplace in Kapa'a.*

Kapa'a Fish & Chowder House $/$$ D, R 822-7488

Extensive variety of excellent seafood, both local and imported, and prime rib. Some Cajun-style dishes are on the menu; New York steak is a specialty. Expensive wine list. Children's entrees available. Reservations are recommended; ask for a table in the Garden Room, a lovely plant-filled, screened lanai, softly lit by candles and lanterns. *1639 Kūhiō Hwy. (mauka side), Kapa'a*

Kaua'i Chop Suey L/D 245-8790

Clean, bright dining room decorated in red and white with Chinese lanterns. Delicious Cantonese specialties at budget-pleasing prices. Take-out orders available; no credit cards accepted. Lunch Tues.-Sat. from 11:00 a.m. to 2:00 p.m., dinner Tues.-Sun. from 4:30-9:00 p.m. *3501 Rice St. (Pacific Ocean Plaza), Līhu'e*

Kiibo Restaurant & Sushi Bar $/$$ L/D   245-2650

Flavorful authentic Japanese fare, with a good variety of choices including tempura, sukiyaki, sushi, sashimi and teriyaki. Photos of the food are on the menu. No credit cards; take-out orders welcome. Open daily: lunch 11:00 a.m. to 1:30 p.m., dinner 5:30 to 9:00 p.m. *2991 Umi St., Līhu'e*

King and I Thai Cuisine $ D, R   822-1642

This cozy family-style restaurant has become a popular dining spot for locals and tourists alike due to its tasty Thai fare and reasonable prices. A good way to start the meal is with their green papaya salad and spring rolls. Nice selection of vegetarian dishes. Friendly service. Open nightly from 4:30 to 9:30 p.m. *4-901 Kūhiō Hwy. (Waipouli Plaza), Kapa'a*

Kintaro Japanese Steak House $$/$$$ D, R   822-3341

Elegant setting and excellent Japanese cuisine with a wide range of sushi, sashimi, tempura plus several beef choices including filet mignon, as well as a teppan yaki area and cocktail lounge. Closed Sundays. *4-370 Kūhiō Hwy., Kapa'a (next to Kinopopo Shopping Village)*

Kountry Kitchen   B/L   822-3511

Great spot for budget-conscious breakfast eaters, known for its design-your-own crepe-like rolled omelettes with many filling choices. The banana pancakes are also good. Booths are comfy and service friendly. Lunch includes salads, sandwiches and burgers. Hot lunch plates include steak, chicken and fish. Lunch items can also be prepared for take-out. This is a popular place, so there may be a wait. Open 6:00 a.m. to 2:30 p.m. *1485 Kūhiō Hwy., Kapa'a*

Mema Cuisine $ and less   L/D   823-0899

Owned by the same owners as King and I Thai Cuisine, this restaurant, specializing in Thai and Chinese cuisine, gets the same good review, offering authentic oriental dishes at modest prices. If two Thai restaurants can operate successfully in such close proximity to each other, they must be doing something right! Lunch served 11:00 a.m. to 2:00 p.m. Monday through Friday; dinner served daily from 5:00 to 9:30 p.m. *361 Kūhiō Hwy., Wailua Shopping Plaza, Kapa'a (next to Sizzler Restaurant)*

Norberto's El Cafe $ and less   D   822-3362

This is Kaua'i's oldest Mexican eatery, highly praised for its tasty cuisine. Cantina decor, with white stucco walls, hanging plants and colorful sombreros. You can order complete dinners or entrees a la carte. Especially noted for its guacamole, homemade salsa (hot!), burritos, tostadas and chilis rellenos. Very friendly service. *4-1373 Kūhiō Hwy., Kapa'a*

Ono Family Restaurant $ and less   B/L/D   822-1710

Generous servings of inexpensive, plain food, with a few interesting, well-prepared house specials. Breakfast is served from 7:00 a.m. daily with dishes ranging from omelettes to tropical pancakes. Local style "plate lunches" are served from 11:00 a.m. to 2:00 p.m. weekdays and 11:30 a.m. to 2:00 p.m. on weekends. The dinner menu includes fresh fish, baby back pork ribs and top sirloin steak (5:30 to 9:00 p.m. nightly). *4-1292 Kūhiō Hwy. (mauka side), Kapa'a*

Papaya's Garden Cafe & Market   L/D   823-0190

If you enjoy healthy eating or just appreciate delicious food, you'll want to check out this casual cafe, with outdoor tables in a pleasant grassy setting complete with a manmade waterfall. Freshly prepared deli salads, sandwiches, soups, pizza, veggie burgers, gourmet vegetarian, chicken, fish and ethnic entrees, as well as desserts. Espresso bar. Serving daily from 10:00 a.m. to 8:00 p.m. *Under the Whale Tower, Kaua'i Village, Kapa'a.*

The Planter's Restaurant $$ D   245-1606

Situated in Hanamā'ulu in a historic sugar plantation building, this restaurant offers steak, seafood and chicken, with prime rib their specialty. The decor is quaint, with interesting artifacts from its former plantation days. The best tables are the two booths next to the waterfall; patio dining is also an option. Children's portions available. Dinner served from 5:00 to 9:30 p.m. *Kūhiō Hwy. (56) in Hanamā'ulu, near mile marker two*

The Tip Top Motel Cafe & Bakery   B/L   245-2333

A bargain hunter's find! This motel has been around since 1916, and the cafe is known for its very reasonable prices. The menu offerings, which include local fare, are simple, but tasty (especially the fresh baked goods). It's a family place, popular with the local residents. The decor is plain, and the booths are comfortable. The cafe is closed Mondays. *3173 Akahi St., Līhu'e*

Tokyo Lobby $/$$ L/D, R   245-8989

Their motto is "the ultimate in Japanese dining". A nice restaurant with good tasty Japanese fare, interesting food presentation, and attentive wait help. Complete with sushi bar. *3501 Rice St. (Pacific Ocean Plaza), Līhu'e*

Wailua Marina Restaurant $/$$ L/D, R   822-4311

Operated by the same family as Hanapēpē's Green Garden Restaurant, this is a nice family place. Situated at Smith's Tropical Paradise on the scenic Wailua River, the extensive menu features steak, seafood and fresh fish. The covered lanai is the most picturesque place to dine, and overlooks the river. Open from 10:30 a.m. to 9:00 p.m. Closed Mondays. *Hwy. 56, Wailua - free shuttle to and from Wailua hotels and condos in the evening*

Waipouli Deli & Restaurant $ and less   B/L/D   822-9311

If you're looking for inexpensive good local food, this is a favorite of Kaua'i residents, and offers American and Oriental dishes served in hearty portions. Their $2.99 breakfast special includes pancakes, eggs and bacon. Lunch and dinner items include seafood plates, an Oriental platter with shrimp tempura, Kaua'i "super saimin" (with ingredients galore) and burgers. Friendly and speedy service. Open daily from 7:00 a.m. to 2:30 p.m., with breakfast served 'til 11:00 a.m.; dinner Fri. & Sat. only from 5:00 p.m. to 9:00 p.m. *Waipouli Town Center, Kapa'a*

South Shore Area Restaurants

Beach House $/$$ B/L/D, R, W   742-1424

The perfect place to watch sunset, this restaurant is situated in a beautiful oceanfront setting. The atmosphere is casual by day, elegant by night. Attractively decorated in hues of burgundy, mauve and teal, the structure was totally remodeled after 1992's Hurricane Iniki. The menu offers steak, seafood, prime rib, and fresh fish. Interesting salads and good desserts emphasize tropical flavors. Open daily, with breakfast served from 7:00 to 11:00 a.m., lunch from 11:00 a.m. to 2:00 p.m., dinner from 5:30 to 9:30 p.m. Separate bar is open from 11:00 a.m. to 10:30 p.m. *5022 Lāwai Rd., Kōloa*

Brennecke's Beach Broiler $/$$ L/D, R   742-7588

This casual, upstairs dining room has a great ocean view overlooking Po'ipū Beach Park, and is a popular family place, known for its fresh fish entrees. Other menu choices include steak, prime rib, Hawaiian spiny lobster, scampi, chicken, ribs, and pasta dishes. Entrees include a trip to the salad bar, sourdough bread, rice or pasta and fresh vegetable. Nice children's menu, reasonably priced. Small, well-selected wine list. The decor is simple, clean and attractive. Consistently good food, affordable prices and attentive service make it a highly recommended south shore establishment. Open daily from 11:30 a.m. to 10:00 p.m. *Ho'one Rd., across from Po'ipū Beach Park, Po'ipū*

Brick Oven Pizza $ and less   L/D   332-8561

The best pizza on Kaua'i--ask anyone. Your tastebuds will applaud. Meat toppings, dough (white or wheat) and other ingredients are all home-made; pizza crust is thin and flavored with garlic butter. Besides great pizza, you'll find hot sandwiches, salads, beer and wine. A cheery, spacious dining room sports the standard red and white checked tablecloths, and children are treated with TLC by the friendly staff. Smoker-free dining. Open Mon.-Sat. from 11:00 a.m. to 10:00 p.m. Closed Sundays. Pizza-to-go available. *2-2555 Kaumuali'i Hwy. (Hwy. 50), mauka side, Kalāheo.*

Camp House Grill $ and less   B/L/D   332-9755

A fun eatery that serves up burgers, hot dogs, fries, milk shakes, barbecued "huli" chicken, steak, pork ribs, fresh fish and desserts. This is another good place to take the kids. Don't be put off by the rustic exterior--the cars in the parking lot prove its popularity and inside it's clean. Kids can color the placemats to their heart's content while awaiting their food. Especially friendly service. *Kaumuali'i Highway (50), Kalāheo.*

Dondero's $$/$$$ D, R   742-1234

An elegantly decorated upscale restaurant located in the Hyatt Regency Kaua'i, boasting inlaid marble flooring, ornate tile work and Franciscan murals of Mediterranean scenes. Weather permitting, you can dine outside under the stars on the piazza or indoors in the attractive dining room, with soft classical music to complement the ambiance. The menu has *a la carte* entrees featuring regional Italian cuisine, with dishes including *gnocci* (potato dumplings), *gamberi con stracci* (lemon shrimp and spinach pasta), *ossobuco, cioppino*, seafood ravioli, rack of lamb, among others. Excellent desserts. Appropriate dress required (casual resort wear, collared shirts for men). *Hyatt Regency Kaua'i, 1571 Po'ipū Rd., Kōloa*

The House of Seafood $$/$$$ D, R   742-6433

Fresh local fish is the specialty of this excellent restaurant, with probably the largest variety of fish available on the island. Try something from the tasty appetizer selection to start. Chowder or salad, homemade rolls, wild rice, and vegetable are included with nicely portioned entrees. Well-chosen, moderately priced wine list; freshly made desserts. Very good children's menu with modest prices; friendly attentive wait help. Decorated with a tropical flair--rattan and lots of live greenery--and tables are spaced for privacy. Serving nightly from 5:30 to 9:30 p.m. *1941 Po'ipū Rd., Po'ipū (at the Po'ipū Kai Resort)*

Ilima Terrace $/$$ B/L/D, R, W   742-1234

Offering relaxed dining in an open-air atmosphere at the Hyatt Regency, this lovely restaurant is set amid koi-filled streams, waterfalls and lush greenery, with beautiful ocean views. This is continental cuisine at its finest. Designed to allow both families and couples their privacy, it is tastefully decorated in a style reminiscent of Old Hawaii's plantation era. A lavish breakfast buffet is served Sundays offering made-to-order omelettes, fresh tropical fruit and juices, assorted baked goods, champagne, and much more. The lunch menu has superb salads, pasta, hot entrees, sandwiches and pizza. Nightly dinner buffets center on a theme--Island Night, Barbecue Night and Prime Rib Night--and are reasonably priced. *Hyatt Regency Kaua'i, 1571 Po'ipū Rd., Kōloa*

Kalaheo Steak House $/$$ D   332-9780

Here you'll find excellent steak, seafood and chicken at quite reasonable prices. Entrees include salad and choice of starch, as well as fresh bread. Dining room is informal, done in knotty pine, with comfortable booths as well as tables. Service staff is attentive and friendly. Wine list is minimal. *4444 Papalina Rd., Kalāheo*

Keoki's Paradise $$ D   742-7534

If Hollywood were to create the definitive tropical island restaurant, it would probably look much like Keoki's Paradise. Tables set in staggered levels around a landscaped lagoon, tiki torches, booths decked out with thatched roofs, rattan chairs and wooden tables, lots of greenery, even a festive taco bar. The menu is primarily steak, chicken and seafood, as well as Mexican dishes. *Po'ipū Shopping Village, Po'ipū*

The Koloa Broiler $ and less   L/D,   R742-9122

If you don't mind a broil-it-yourself meal, this can be a fun experience, especially for families with children. Steak, fish, kabobs, ribs and burgers are the standard fare, and the prices will please the budget-conscious. The large dining room is simple, with a casual atmosphere. Meals come with all-you-can-eat salad, rice, baked beans and sourdough bread. Open daily; closed Thanksgiving Day and Christmas Day. *Situated right in the middle of Old Kōloa Town*

Roy's Poipu Bar & Grill $/$$ D, R, W   742-5000

Talented chef Roy Yamaguchi's sixth and newest restaurant (he also has locations in Oahu, Maui, Guam and Tokyo) opened its doors in November of 1994, carrying on his fine tradition of gourmet Euro-Asian-Pacific cuisine. Specializing in fresh fish, the menu also offers steaks, seafood, chicken, lamb and pasta, with specials changing nightly. The casually elegant restaurant is enclosed in glass, which may be opened for al fresco dining or closed, depending on weather conditions and season, and an open kitchen allows patrons to catch a glimpse of culinary artistry in progress. An attractive color scheme combines rich sapphire blue, emerald green and deep rust. Dinner is served nightly from 5:30 to 9:30 p.m. Reservations recommended. *Po'ipū Shopping Village, Po'ipū*

Taqueria Nortenos   L/D   742-7222

Some consider this the best place for Mexican food on Kaua'i. Eat in or take out. Prices are cheap; you can eat for less than five dollars and not go away hungry. Generous portions and the food is fresh, with no skimping on ingredients. Vegetarian selections also available. It's a popular place, so you may find yourself standing in line. Closed Wednesdays. *2827-A Po'ipū Road, Po'ipū Plaza*

Tidepools	$/$$	D, R, W	742-1234

Situated in the middle of a tranquil lagoon at the Hyatt Regency Kaua'i, this seafood restaurant is divided into small grass-thatched huts for intimate dining. Wood-plank rope bridges connect these private shelters overlooking the lagoon, with views of the pool and waterfalls. Tiki torches enhance the romantic setting, creating a truly tropical dining experience. Specialties include fresh Pacific seafood with a Polynesian flair, charbroiled steaks, prime rib, roasted chicken, in addition to local favorites like charred ahi sashimi and grilled mahi-mahi. There's even a cozy lounge--a nice place to watch sunset and enjoy a tropical drink before dinner. *Hyatt Regency Kaua'i, 1571 Po'ipū Rd., Kōloa*

Southwest Shore Area Restaurants

The Espresso Bar	$ and less	B/L/D, R	335-8544

(Hanapēpē Bookstore)

On your way to or from Waimea, this is a good place to stop for a vegetarian meal, hot cup of espresso or cappuccino, or to satisfy your sweet tooth. Breakfast features items such as multi-grain waffles or pancakes (with real maple syrup), baked frittata and other healthy fare. Lunch offers soups, salads, sandwiches, pasta and veggie burgers, as well as homemade desserts. For dinner, choose from four gourmet Italian vegetarian entrees, made with fresh local produce. Breakfast and lunch served Wednesday through Sunday from 8:00 a.m to 3:00 p.m.; dinner served Thursday through Saturday from 6:00 to 9:30 p.m. with live music (Hawaiian slack key or classical guitar). The bookstore has a wide selection of Hawaiiana books, tropical lotions, soaps and potpourri, and other gift items. *3830 Hanapēpē Rd., Hanapēpē*

Green Garden	$/$$	B/L/D, W	335-5422

This popular family-run restaurant, in operation since 1948, is another good choice for satisfying your appetite on your way to or from sight-seeing at Waimea Canyon. It's constantly crowded due to its wide menu selection of excellent, inexpensive food served in generously-sized portions. Entree specialties (there are more than twenty) parallel Hawai'i's diverse ethnic makeup, and include Hawaiian, Portuguese, Japanese, Chinese and American dishes. A scrumptious assortment of homemade pies to choose from-- *liliko'i* (passion fruit) is the favorite, with macadamia nut cream and coconut cream pies tied for second. Service is fast and friendly. Closed Tuesdays. *13949 Kaumuali'i Hwy. (50), Hanapēpē*

Many tasty ethnic food are available on Kaua'i.

The Grove Dining Room $/$$ L/D, R, E   338-2300

Set in a scenic coconut grove, this casual plantation-style restaurant is one of the few places to eat in Waimea, and a good choice for lunch, dinner or Sunday brunch. Tables are set on an open-air lanai overlooking a lovely lawn and garden area, with stately coconut trees and quaint restored Hawaiian plantation cottages. The menu changes daily and offers steaks, fresh island fish, seafood, chicken and ribs. A children's *(keiki)* menu is also available. Live music is presented on Fridays and Saturdays, featuring a local Hawaiian trio. Lunch is served Tuesday through Saturday from 11:30 a.m. to 2:30 p.m.; dinner is served Tuesday through Sunday starting at 4:30 p.m. Sunday brunch runs from 10:00 a.m to 2:00 p.m., offering a lavish spread including made-to-order omelettes, prime rib, baked ham, fish, fruits, salads and desserts. The brunch is reasonably priced, with discounts available to senior citizens and children age twelve and under. *9400 Kaumuali'i Hwy. (makai side, between mile markers 23 and 24), Waimea*

Kokee Lodge   B/L   335-6061

Set in a peaceful 4,345-acre wilderness preserve halfway between Waimea Canyon and Kalalau Valley Lookout, at an elevation of 3600 feet, this rustic lodge is open daily for breakast and lunch. Breakfast is served from 9:00 a.m., featuring light fare such as assorted muffins, cornbread and quiche; lunch is available from 10:30 a.m. until 3:30 p.m., offering soup, salads, chili, sandwiches, and dessert items. Meal prices are modest; food is hearty and good. The gift shop is well-stocked with made-in-Hawai'i souvenirs. Allow time to visit the museum next door, which has a number of interesting, informative exhibits. *3600 Kōke'e Rd., on the way to Waimea Canyon*

North Shore Area Restaurants

Bali Hai Restaurant $/$$ B/L/D, R, E   826-6522

If you want a fabulous view of sunset over Hanalei Bay, be sure and arrive at this casual clifftop restaurant before the sun goes down. Or, if you'd like to enjoy breakfast or lunch with a breathtaking view of the north shore, you won't find a better place. The dining room was recently redecorated with attractive teak furniture and gem-hued fabrics of purple and turquoise. The structure is open-air on three sides with a high *lauhala* (plaited pandanus leaves) ceiling, allowing expansive vistas of Hanalei Bay and Hāena. The dinner menu offers Pacific Rim cuisine and features fresh local fish, seafood, steaks and chicken, with child portions available on fish entrees. Their two chefs are creative in food presentation, using locally grown produce and interesting seasonings in most dishes. Nightly entertainment in the Happy Talk Lounge. *Hanalei Bay Resort, Princeville*

116

Black Pot Luau Hut $/$$ L/D 826-9871

This small family-run Hanalei restaurant is probably the best place for Hawaiian food in north shore. Its menu is varied and reflects the popular local entrees. If you can't quite decide what kind of food you're in the mood for, you are at the right place. It offers Hawaiian (*kalua* pig, *lau lau*, *lomi lomi*), Chinese (stir-fried dishes, saimin), Mexican and Filipino food, American burgers as well as fresh fish. And as a special treat for vegetarian, owner/chef Cathy Ham Young offers stir-fried fresh vegetables which are hand-picked from her farm each morning. *Aku Rd, Hanalei, around the corner from Ching Young Village*

Cafe Hanalei and Terrace $/$$-B/L, $$/$$$-D 826-9644

With spectacular views of Hanalei Bay and the mountains, any meal here is a delightful experience. Seating is available indoors or out, and the menu features an abundant array of Pacific Rim creations. Breakfast buffets are offered daily, limited only by your imagination. Menu items include whole wheat pancakes with macadamia nuts and guava syrup, and interesting omelettes. Luncheon fare offers such dishes as grilled vegetables with baked goat cheese, fresh salads, and all-American hamburgers. Dinner choices include seared ahi, grilled steaks and fresh island fish, as well as Japanese specialties. Theme dinner buffets are also presented, and a brunch buffet is featured on Sunday. Attentive service. *Princeville Hotel, Princeville*

Casa di Amici $$/$$$ L/D, R, W, E 828-1388

This charming Italian restaurant (its name means "house of friends") is situated in picturesque Kīlauea. Its beautiful dining room is decorated in dark green hues, with candlelit tables, wicker chairs, clay fountain, and glass doors that slide open for breezy *al fresco* dining. Several types of pasta dishes are offered in large or "light" portions topped with a variety of sauces, as well as fresh fish, chicken and veal entrees. Good salads, tasty baked bread and nice selection of Italian wines. Excellent service. Live piano music most evenings. *2484 Keneke St. at Lighthouse Rd., Kīlauea (next to Kong Lung Co. store)*

Charo's Restaurant and Bar $/$$ L/D, R, E 826-6422

Situated oceanfront at Hāena, and owned by flamboyant ("cuchi-cuchi") Latin entertainer, Charo, a part-time Kaua'i resident, this attractive restaurant was completely remodeled after sustaining damage in 1992's Hurricane Iniki, and reopened for business in July of '94. Although not serving their full menu as of this writing, it will likely be operating once again at full throttle in 1995, offering Mexican and Continental cuisine and fresh fish as their specialties. Live entertainment is featured on certain nights, so call for the latest update and for reservations. This is also a picturesque place to relax, have a margarita and watch sunset. *Adjacent to Hanalei Colony Resort, 5-7132 Kūhiō Hwy., Hāena*

Chuck's Steak House $/$$ L/D, R 826-6211

Paniolos (cowboys) will feel right at home here. The place has simple
Western decor, and an extensive menu selection of steaks, barbecued ribs,
prime rib, seafood and chicken. A children's menu is also available. Lunch
features large delicious hamburgers, hot dogs, ribs and steak sandwiches.
The place is comfortable, the food is moderately priced and flavorful, and its
a nice family place. *Princeville Shopping Center, Hanalei.*

Hanalei Dolphin Restaurant and Fish Market $$ D 826-6113

The oldest restaurant on the north shore, located on the Hanalei River
with a rustic setting and open air dining. This is a popular place, small and
usually crowded, so get there early, as they do not take reservations. Fresh
fish is their specialty, as well as steak and chicken, and dinners include salad
and fresh bread. Try the seafood chowder to start, which is creamy, tasty
and not skimpy on ingredients. Good wine list, friendly service. Children's
menu available. Smoke-free dining; open from 5:30 to 10:00 p.m. *Hwy. 56,
Hanalei*

The Hanalei Gourmet $ and less B/L/D, E 826-2524

Their motto is "risky cookery at its best". This popular deli-style gourmet
kitchen is situated in an old schoolhouse in Hanalei, and is a great place to
pick up a box lunch for daytime excursions. You can also eat in the cafe, or
on their open-air veranda. Featuring deli fare, fresh home-baked breads,
soups, generously-sized sandwiches, salads, pastry items, gourmet foods and
wine. The small cafe/bar is a converted classroom, and comes alive after
dark with live music most nights, pupus and drinks. Full tropical bar and
on-site bakery. A north shore favorite, open daily from 8:00 a.m. to 10:00
p.m. *5-5161 Kūhiō Hwy. (Hanalei Center), Hanalei*

La Cascata Restaurant $$/$$$ D, R, E 826-2761

A lovely restaurant in the Princeville Hotel, with a picturesque view of
Hanalei Bay. The menu features authentic Italian and French Riviera cuisine,
and the decor boasts scenic hand-painted murals, double-vaulted ceiling, and
quarry tile floors. Entrees include interesting pasta dishes with sauces on the
light side, fresh seafood, chicken, and beef. Attentive service; well-selected,
expensive wine list. Entertainment Wednesday through Sunday. Great
sunset view! *Princeville Hotel, Princeville*

Tahiti Nui B/L/D $/$$-D R, E 826-6277

A bit of old Kaua'i in the heart of Hanalei, this charming restaurant and
lounge is a great place to relax, enjoy Hawaiian cuisine and "talk story" with
local residents, who frequent the place. The food is inexpensive local fare,
with the dinner menu featuring steak, fresh fish, chicken and ribs. A luau
and show is presented on Wednesdays and Fridays, with authentic entertainment and food at a reasonable price. It's also a nice place to just sit down and
have a drink in the bar. *Kūhiō Hwy. (56), Hanalei*

Tropical Taco   L/D   826-6878

This is the famous green van with a colorful surfboard sign you'll see parked at the entrance to Hanalei, offering very good take-out Mexican fare. It's a popular landmark, in business on the island since '78. Menu items feature their *piece de resistance* "Tropical Taco", as well as tostadas, burritos, and beer-battered fresh fish-of-the-day. If you find yourself scurrying from here to there on the north shore, and are in the mood for some good Mexican fast food, this is a great pick. Open daily from 11:00 a.m. to 3:00 p.m. *Hanalei--look for the green van on the right as you enter town*

Winds of Beamreach $/$$ D, R   826-6143

"Beamreach" is a sailing term, and was this restaurant's former name. With a new name and a fresh new look (it closed as a result of 1992's Hurricane Iniki), it's up and running once again. The menu features a nice selection of pupus (appetizers), and entrees include steaks and seafood, as well as fresh fish, a nightly pasta special, and stir-fry dishes, which are served with salad, roasted potato or rice. The ambiance is Hawaiian, and the dining room is decorated with *lauhala* (plaited pandanus leaf) mats, authentic Hawaiian fishing baskets and artwork from local artists, with touches of live greenery. Ask about their "Sunset Special", priced nightly and served from 5:30 to 6:30 p.m. The dining room affords a mountain view, and is totally non-smoking, with smoking allowed only in the bar. Reservations required. Open nightly, with cocktails from 4:30 p.m. and dinner served from 5:30 p.m. *Pali Ke Kua Resort, Princeville*

118

FAST FOODS

A fun place to take the kids is a mustard-yellow hot dog emporium called **Mustard's Last Stand**, offering a dozen delicious varieties of this sausage treat, with a salad-bar size condiment counter where you pile on your choice of many toppings. It even has its own miniature golf course, as well as live ducks and rabbits roaming about a Japanese-style koi (carp) pond. There's also a big simulated wave and surfboard to snap a fun "hang ten" family photo to take home. Located in Lāwai, corner of Kōloa Road (530) at Kaumuali'i Hwy. (50) - (332-7245).

Duane's Ono Char-Burger is considered the best burger place on Kaua'i, offering a tasty selection of burgers, fries and shakes. Located in Anahola, on the northeast shore - (822-9181).

Bubba's Burgers has two restaurants on the island, and is a local favorite. Located in Kapa'a (823-0069) or Hanalei (826-7839).

Kīlauea Bakery & Pau Hana Pizza is a small place with limited indoor and outdoor seating. Pau Hana features interesting, flavorful pizzas with unusual toppings, available whole or by the slice. The pizza portion is open from 11:00 a.m. to 9:00 p.m.; the bakery is open from 6:30 a.m. to 9:00 p.m. Both are closed Sundays. Located at Kong Lung Center, Kīlauea - 828-2020.

If you have access to an oven, **Paradise Pizza** in Kapa'a (823-8253) offers "take 'n bake" pizza, with numerous interesting toppings to choose from, and dough made fresh daily. A family of four can eat here for under twenty dollars. Open Tuesday through Sunday, 3:00 to 8:00 p.m. Located behind Safeway at Kauai Village, Kapa'a.

Mainland fast food giants are sprinkled throughout the islands as follows: **Burger King** - Kap'aa Shopping Ctr., and 4440 Kukui Grove (Līhu'e); **Dairy Queen** - 4302 Rice St. (Līhu'e), Eleele Center, and in Waimea; **Domino's Pizza** - 3100 Kūhiō Hwy. (Līhu'e); **Jack in the Box** - 3160 Kūhiō Hwy. (Līhu'e); **Kentucky Fried Chicken** - 3229 Kūhiō Hwy. (Līhu'e), and 4-919 Kūhiō Hwy. (Kapa'a); **McDonald's** - 3-3113 Kūhiō Hwy. (Līhu'e) and 4-0771 Kūhiō Hwy. (Kapa'a); **Pizza Hut** - 3-3171 Kūhiō Hwy. (Līhu'e) and Waipouli Town Center; **Sizzler** - 4361 Kūhiō Hwy. (Kapa'a), **Taco Bell** - 4-927 Kūhiō Hwy. (Kapa'a) and 4422 Kukui Grove (Līhu'e).

ICE CREAM and FROZEN YOGURT

The premier ice cream vendor in Kaua'i is **Lappert's Ice Cream,** which began as a small shop in Hanapēpē and has become so successful that it has expanded throughout Kaua'i and all the Hawaiian islands, and even to California. It has four stores on the island--in Hanapēpē, Princeville, Coconut Marketplace and Kōloa.

Mainland chain ice cream stores on the island are **Baskin Robbins 31 Flavors**, located in Lihu'e Town Center (4-831 Kūhiō Hwy.), and **Dairy Queen,** which has three locations--Līhu'e, Eleele and Waimea.

For those who prefer frozen yogurt over ice cream, there is **TCBY Yogurt** in Līhu'e, at 4-361 Kūhiō Hwy. **Zack's Famous Frozen Yogurt and Cafe** has two locations, one in Kukui Grove Center and another in Coconut Marketplace

SHAVE ICE

The refreshing treat known as 'shave ice' can't be packed and shipped home from Kaua'i. Finely-shaved ice with flavored syrup poured over it, this cool thirst-quencher closely resembles what is generally known on the Mainland as 'snow cones', but it *isn't* the same. The texture of shave ice is much finer--more like actual snow, and the rainbow version is a delight to behold as well as to consume. On a hot afternoon, this treat is ultra-refreshing. Some vendors will add a scoop of ice cream or sweet red beans (also known as azuki beans) under the mound of delicate ice shavings for an extra treat. Shave ice can be purchased from many places all over the island, including refreshment vans parked near beaches.

DINING

ESPRESSO BARS

If you want to perk up with a steaming cup of fresh roasted brew, there are several coffee houses on every side of the island to quash your caffeine fever. On the north shore, in Hanalei, there's the quaint **Old Hanalei Coffee Company,** featuring Kona espresso and cappuccino. They also serve a light breakfast, lunch and fix made-to-order picnic baskets, as well as home-made baked goods. Located at Hanalei Center (826-6717).

Papaya's Garden Cafe in Kapa'a provides tables in a refreshing outdoor setting, offering espresso and an array of fine coffees, as well as fresh bakery items and a full gourmet deli (see "Restaurants, East Shore"). Located at Kauai Village, Kapa'a (823-0190).

On the southwest side of the island is **The Espresso Bar,** in the Hanapēpē Bookstore, offering espresso, cappuccino, cafe latte, coffee mocha, Kona Gourmet and locally grown Kauai Island coffees, as well as fresh juices, herbal teas, home-made pastries, and vegetarian meals (see "Restaurants, Southwest Shore"). Located at 3830 Hanapēpē Rd., Hanapēpē (335-5011)

In Kalāheo, on the south shore, you'll find the **Kalaheo Coffee Co. & Cafe,** providing coffees from around the world, including Hawaiian, flavored and international blends. Breakfast and lunch are also served. Located at the traffic light in Kalāheo (332-5858).

NUTS, CANDIES and JAMS

One of Hawai'i's famous edibles is the macadamia nut, brought to the islands from Australia, and the succulent kernels are available roasted and salted or laced with an imaginative array of coatings--in addition to the standard chocolate,

coffee and honey--in many gift and souvenir shops all over the island. A specialist in these as well as other sweet treats, like tropical fruit jams, jellies and syrups, is **The Nut Cracker Sweet** (822-4811) at Coconut Market-place.

BAKED GOODS

The spreading of fame of the **Kaua'i Kookie Kompany** of Hanapēpē (their products can be bought in most grocery stores on Kaua'i and throughout the state), has sparked competition by other island bakers. You may want to stop in at **Popo's** cookie store as you pass through Kapa'a, another favorite local cookie company. Even **Lappert's** of Hanapēpē ice cream fame has gotten into the act with a line of clones that should bring a

worried furrow to the brow of Mrs. Fields. In addition to cookies, Lappert's Old Kōloa Town shop produces, cinnamon rolls, danish and muffins that are worth going out of your way for and they have a few tables on a patio area if you wish to eat on the spot.

Kaua'i also seems to be running a competition for the world's best *liliko'i* (passion fruit) chiffon pie. Many restaurants bake their own and some sell whole pies. Among the strongest contenders for the title are **Omoide Bakery and Delicatessen** and **Green Garden** both in Hanapepe. **Kaua'i Kitchens** specializes in *malasadas* (soft sugared doughnuts without a hole) and Portuguese sweet bread; it has three locations--Kōloa, Rice Shopping Center (Lihu'e) and Waimea. The **Tip Top Bakery** in Lihu'e bakes a delightful variety of breads and pastries. The **Village Snack and Bake Shop** in Hanalei's Ching Young Village, **Kapa'a Bakery** (Kapa'a Shopping Center) and **Garden Isle Bake Shop** in Pacific Ocean Plaza, across from the Kaua'i Marriott in Lihu'e, also offer a wide range of scrumptious baked goodies.

COOKBOOKS

Those doing their own cooking might wish to try some local recipes, taking advantage of the readily available ingredients, which can be hard to come by in some areas and climates. Many such cookbooks are sold at local bookstores and souvenir shops. Island Heritage Publishing has published three collections of local recipes which we can recommend: *Favorite Recipes from Hawaii*, *Tropical Drinks and Pupus from Hawaii*, and *Entertaining Island Style*. All three are available in hard or soft cover.

GUIDE TO FRESH ISLAND FISH

When a waitperson in a Hawai'i restaurant rattles off a selection of island fish on the menu, do you get confused? Sometimes the names of island fish tend to blend together, so here's a guide to a few of the most popular varieties.

AHI: Also known as yellowfin tuna, this fish may weigh anywhere between 10 and 250 pounds. Its firm unfishy flesh is eaten raw, as sashimi, or broiled in thick filets.

AU: This is the familiar swordfish, which comes in many varieties that are great for eating. It has a white flesh similar to the mahimahi.

MAHIMAHI: This fish is probably the most popular on Hawaiian tables. It's known as the "dolphin fish", but it is definitely a fish and not the marine mammal known as the dolphin. Mahimahi has a flaky texture and a mild taste.

ONO: Another name for this fish is the "wahoo". It's a fast swimmer and can clip along at sixty miles per hour! To give you some idea of how it tastes, "ono" means delicious in Hawaiian.

ONAGA: Red snapper. Its white meat is used for sashimi. This pretty pink fish is sometimes used as a table ornament.

OPAKAPAKA: Another snapper, this one dwells in fairly deep water and isn't easy to catch. But its melt-in-the-mouth deliciousness makes it worth the trouble!

Fish guide provided courtesy of Kauai Beach Press

If you have access to an oven, **Paradise Pizza** in Kapa'a (823-8253) offers "take 'n bake" pizza, with numerous interesting toppings to choose from, and dough made fresh daily. You can feed a family of four for under twenty dollars. Open Tuesday through Sunday, 3:00 to 8:00 p.m. Located behind Safeway at Kauai Village, Kapa'a.

Mainland fast food giants are sprinkled throughout the islands as follows:

Burger King - Kap'aa Shopping Ctr., and 4440 Kukui Grove (Lihu'e)

Dairy Queen- 4302 Rice St. (Lihu'e), Eleele Center, and in Waimea.

Domino's Pizza - 3100 Kūhiō Hwy. (Lihu'e)

Jack in the Box - 3160 Kūhiō Hwy. (Lihu'e)

Kentucky Fried Chicken - 3229 Kūhiō Hwy. (Lihu'e), and 4-919 Kūhiō Hwy. (Kapa'a)

McDonald's - 3-3113 Kūhiō Hwy. (Lihu'e) and 4-0771 Kūhiō Hwy. (Kapa'a)

Pizza Hut - 3-3171 Kūhiō Hwy. (Lihu'e) and Waipouli Town Center

Sizzler - 4361 Kūhiō Hwy. (Kapa'a)

Taco Bell - 4-927 Kūhiō Hwy. (Kapa'a) and 4422 Kukui Grove (Lihu'e).

ICE CREAM and FROZEN YOGURT

The premier ice cream vendor in Kaua'i is **Lappert's Ice Cream**, which began as a small shop in Hanapēpē and has become so successful that it has expanded throughout Kaua'i and all the Hawaiian islands, and even to California. It has four stores on the island--in Hanapēpē, Princeville, Coconut Marketplace and Kōloa.

Mainland chain ice cream stores on the island are **Baskin Robbins 31 Flavors**, located in Lihu'e Town Center (4-831 Kūhiō Hwy.), and **Dairy Queen,** which has three locations--Lihu'e, Eleele and Waimea.

For those who prefer frozen yogurt over ice cream, there is **TCBY Yogurt** in Lihu'e, at 4-361 Kūhiō Hwy.

Zack's Famous Frozen Yogurt and Cafe has two locations, one in Kukui Grove Center and another in Coconut Marketplace

SHAVE ICE

The refreshing treat known as 'shave ice' can't be packed and shipped home from Kaua'i. Finely-shaved ice with flavored syrup poured over it, this cool thirst-quencher closely resembles what is generally known on the Mainland as 'snow cones', but it *isn't* the same. The texture of shave ice is much finer--more like actual snow, and the rainbow version is a delight to behold as well as to consume. On a hot afternoon, this treat is ultra-refreshing. Some vendors will add a scoop of ice cream or sweet black beans under the mound of delicate ice shavings for an extra treat. Shave ice can be purchased from many places all over the island, including refreshment vans parked near beaches.

ACCOMMODATION

Hotels and Condominiums
Bed & Breakfast Homes
Cabins and Campsites
Cottages

ACCOMMODATION

Kaua'i's best hotels are described and rated below, followed by notations and other types of lodging. While most people think automatically of hotels and condominiums when seeking a place to stay for their vacations, there are, in fact, several alternatives--such as vacation homes, bed and breakfast lodging, cottages and camping cabins.

THE BEST HOTELS ON KAUA'I

The ratings below indicate the quality of selected hotels on Kaua'i. The criteria for a good hotel are simple: comfort, courtesy and cleanliness. In a great hotel, different things make different properties outstanding; our evaluations are based on the following criteria:

- architecture, decor, grounds and view
- well-trained, responsible and caring staff
- personalized consideration from manager, concierge and maitre d', prompt room service, attention to details
- amenities and niceties such as fluffy towels, extra pillows, newspaper and wake-up coffee, flowers, beauty salons and shops
- fine dining, all-day restaurant and food service, poolside grazing
- most importantly, an indefinable, warm, pleasing ambiance

Unless you're traveling during the busy winter months (December through April; peak at January) or July and August, reservations shouldn't be a problem. Room rates are seasonal, with the winter months fetching higher prices. The price ranges of the hotels and other lodging are categorized as follows:

$$$$	$200 and more (luxury class)
$$$	$100-$200
$$	$70-$100
$	$50-$70
No $	Under $50 (budget)
W	Wheelchair access

Many luxury class hotels on Kaua'i offer comfort and elegence to distinguished guests.

Aston Kauai Beachboy Hotel	$-/$$$	800-922-7866 808-822-3441

Waipouli beachfront, 243 rooms, 100% air-conditioned, two swimming pools, wading pool, beach, volleyball, tennis, restaurant, two lounges, adjacent shopping village, nearby golf course. Children under 18 yrs. in parents' room no charge with existing bedding. *Coconut Plantation, 4-484 Kūhiō Hwy., Kapa'a (Fax: 808-922-8785)*

Coco Palms Resort $$-$$$$ 808-822-4921

Closed after Hurricane Iniki in 1992, no reopening date has yet been set as of this writing. Romantic setting in coconut grove, 390 rooms, cottages and suites, 100% air-conditioned. Three pools, nine tennis courts, two paddle tennis courts, wedding chapel, shops, restaurant, beauty salon. Across from Wailua Beach. Wedding chapel currently available for ceremonies. *4-241 Kūhiō Hwy., Wailua (Fax: 822-7189)*

Garden Island Inn	$/$$, W	800-648-0154 808-245-7227

Opposite Nāwiliwili Park, just two miles from Līhu'e airport, and within a short walking distance from Kalapaki Beach (a safe swimming beach) and a number of restaurants and shops. 21 bright oceanview rooms can accommodate two guests, with a few larger rooms suitable for up to four people. All rooms have ceiling fans, small refrigerators, microwaves, phones, wet bars, color cable TV, coffee makers and complimentary Kona coffee, with daily maid service. Ground floor rooms are wheelchair accessible. *3445 Wilcox Rd., Līhu'e (Fax same as phone: 245-7227)*

Hanalei Bay Resort	$$$-$$$$, W	800-827-4427 (in HI.) 800-221-6061

Princeville, overlooking stunning Hanalei Bay. 120 hotel rooms and 75 one-, two- and three-bedroom apartments, many with ocean views, 100% air-conditioned, with golf, tennis, swimming pools, restaurant (Bali Hai), cocktail lounge (Happy Talk), shops, beauty salon, laundry facilities. (Also see Embassy Suites Kauai under "Condominiums") *5380 Honoiki Rd., Princeville (Fax: 808-826-6680, property phone: 808-826-6522)*

Hanalei Inn $/$$ 808-826-9333

This quaint rustic inn is situated just one short block from Hanalei Bay. Four mountain-view units are available, each with hardwood floors, full kitchen, private bath, ceilng fans and cable TV. The building is plantation style, and guests can enjoy breathtaking waterfalls from the outdoor lanai. An outdoor thatch-roofed patio area has gas barbecue and swings. Rooms have no phone, however, guests may share an outdoor phone. *P. O. Box 1373, Hanalei, Hawai'i 96714*

Hotel Coral Reef	$/$$, W	800-843-4659 808-822-4481

Small, friendly tropical hotel, beachfront at Kapa'a. 26 rooms (16 oceanfront; 10 non-oceanfront, most of which are oceanview). Oceanfront rooms are 50 yards from the beach, with small refrigerators, color televisions, large sliding glass doors and private lanais. Two mountainview suites are due to open in 1995. Some rooms have wheelchair access. Public swimming pool within walking distance, public tennis courts nearby, Wailua Golf Course is a ten-minute drive; shops and restaurants are close by. Children under 12 stay free with parents, using existing bedding. Activities desk and complimentary coffee in lobby. *1516 Kūhiō Hwy., Kapa'a*

Hyatt Regency Kauai Resort & Spa	$$$$, W	800-233-1234 808-742-1234

Built in a classic 1920s style Hawaiian architecture, this magnificent resort is surrounded by formal gardens, open-air courtyards, peaceful saltwater lagoons, situated overlooking Keoneloa Bay on Kaua'i's south shore. Its 598 rooms (70% offer ocean view) are decorated with rattan wood furnishing and have large, private lanais, separate sitting areas, elegant bathrooms with double marble sinks, in-room safes and other amenities. Fabulous swimming pools, complete with a 150-foot water slide, waterfalls and Jacuzzis, as well as swimmable saltwater lagoons. "Camp Hyatt" is their children's daily activity program for ages 3-12, (from 9:15 a.m. to 4:00 p.m., available for an extra fee). 18-hole championship golf course, designed by Robert Trent Jones, Jr., four tennis courts, five restaurants and lounges, the luxurious 25,000 square-foot Anara Spa, an intimate art deco themed nightclub (Kuhio's), kids' video room, retail shops, horse stables, and extensive banquet facilities. *1571 Po'ipū Rd., Kōloa (Fax: 808-742-6229)*

Islander on the Beach	$-$$$	800-847-7417 808-822-7417

Beachfront at Wailua Beach, 196 rooms, equipped with refrigerators, coffee makers, air-conditioning, and television. Additionally, oceanfront rooms have microwaves and private lanais. Grounds feature six acres of tropical gardens and 500 feet of beach, as well as a swimming pool, Jacuzzi, poolside bar and shops. Activities desk on premises. *4-484 Kūhiō Hwy., Kapa'a (Fax: 808-822-1947)*

Kauai Coconut Beach Resort	$-$$$$, W	800-222-5642 808-822-3455

Waipouli beachfront, in the Kapa'a-Wailua area. Beautifully landscaped grounds in Coconut Plantation. 300 air-conditioned, reasonably priced rooms with private lanais, island-influenced furnishings, plantation shutters, refrigerators, coffee makers with free coffee, color cable televisions and in-room movies. On-site features include swimming pool, three tennis courts (free), Jacuzzi, snack bar, shuffleboard, cocktail lounge, restaurant, meeting rooms and wedding gazebo. Award-winning luau and Polynesian show every night but Friday (see ENTERTAINMENT). Wailua Golf Course is nearby, and other outdoor activities. Rates include rental car and complimentary daily breakfast buffet. *Coconut Plantation, Kapa'a (FAX: 808-822-1830)*

Kauai Marriott	$$-$$$$, W	800-228-9290 808-245-5050

Beachfront setting overlooking Nāwiliwili Bay on the 800-acre Kauai Lagoons resort. Scheduled to reopen in July of 1995. 355 hotel rooms, including 11 suites, and 232 one- and two-bedroom timeshare units. Two Jack Nicklaus designed golf courses, eight tennis courts, lagoons and inland waterways upon which outrigger canoes and mahogany launches travel, horse-drawn carriages, and exotic wildlife. Swimming pool, five Jacuzzis, twelve restaurants and lounges. *Kalapakī Beach, Līhu'e (FAX: 808-245-5049)*

Kauai Resort Hotel	$-$$$$	808-245-3931

Oceanfront at the mouth of the Wailua River on ten lushly landscaped acres. A short walk from Kaua'i's only protected cove, safe for swimming and snorkeling. 228 air-conditioned rooms, each featuring refrigerator, cable television, and in-room movies. Studios and one-bedroom cottages have kitchenettes. Two swimming pools, jet-spa, tennis courts, barbecue area, restaurant, lounge, and Japanese garden. Jogging paths and golf course nearby. *3-5920 Kūhiō Hwy., Kapa'a (Fax: 808-533-0472)*

Kauai Sands	$$, W	800-367-7000 808-822-4951

Waipouli beachfront hotel, situated seven miles from Lihu'e airport. 200 rooms, two swimming pools, white sand beach, oceanfront restaurant (Al & Don's), shops and activities desk. Adjacent to shopping center (Coconut Marketplace), with nearby golf course (Wailua), tennis courts (Coco Palms) and walking/jogging grass boardwalk. Air-conditioned rooms have cable color televisions, refrigerators, ceiling fans and private lanais. *420 Papaloa Rd., Wailua (FAX: 808-922-0052)*

Outrigger Kauai Beach Hotel	$$$/$$$$, W	800-462-6262 808-245-1955

Situated on 25 acres oceanfront, with 350 air-conditioned rooms in a lush tropical garden setting with cascading waterfalls, live exotic birds, a "rock scape" pool and lovely white sand beach. Rooms have large lanais, color televisions, refrigerators and in-room movies. Two restaurants and lounges, two adult pools, large baby pool, whirlpool/spa, four tennis courts. Near Wailua Golf Course. Non-smoking rooms and "family plan" available. *4331 Kaua'i Beach Dr., Līhu'e (Fax: 800-622-4852; 808-246-9085)*

Poipu Beach Resort	$$-$$$$, W	800-468-3571 808-742-1681

Beachfront, 136 rooms, air-conditioning, beach, swimming pool, six tennis courts, shops, restaurants and lounges; nearby golf course and shopping village. Closed after Hurricane Iniki, this resort, as of this writing, has not yet reopened. *2249 Po'ipū Rd., Kōloa*

Princeville, on the edge of Hanalei Bay

Princeville Hotel	$$$$, W	800-826-4400 808-826-9644

This luxurious clifftop landmark overlooks Hanalei Bay, and is situated at the posh 9,000-acre Princeville Resort. Voted by Conde Nast Traveler readers as the eighth best tropical resort in the world (1993), it is elegantly decorated in the fine European tradition. Its luxurious 252 rooms feature custom-designed furnishings, original artwork, in-house movie system, mini bar/pantry and lavish bathrooms with marble double vanities, gold-plated fixtures, lighted makeup mirrors and over-sized tubs. Oceanfront rooms and suites are even more opulent, with extensive use of marble and bathrooms like you might find in a Roman villa. There is a spectacular all-glass lobby, an enlarged oceanside swimming pool, three Jacuzzis, three restaurants, a 66-seat in-house cinema, and a workout room. For sports activities, the Princeville Resort has twenty tennis courts, two top-ranked golf courses and a full health club and spa (see SPORTS), and a number of ocean activities can be arranged at neighboring Hanalei. Shopping is nearby at the Princeville Shopping Center. Vacation packages available. *P. O. Box 3040, Princeville, Hawai'i 96722 (FAX: 808-826-1166)*

ACCOMMODATION

129

Sheraton Kaua'i Resort	$$$/$$$$, W	800-325-3535 808-742-1661

Beachfront at Po'ipū, 456 air-conditioned rooms and suites, two lagoons, two swimming pools, restaurants and lounges. Currently under renovation and not yet fully reopened since closing down after Hurricane Iniki in 1992. *Po'ipū Beach*

Stouffer Wai'ohai Beach Resort	$$$/$$$$, W	800-468-3571 808-742-9511

Beachfront, 426 rooms and 21 luxury suites; air-conditioning, three swimming pools, wading pool, beach, fitness center, six tennis courts, adjacent golf course, restaurants, lounge, shops. It has been closed since September, 1992 after being hard-hit by Hurricane Iniki. No reopening date has been announced, as of this writing. The resort may be renamed due to recent acquisition by the owners of Renaissance Hotels International, which purchased the entire Stouffer chain. *2249 Po'ipū Rd., Po'ipū*

Tip Top Motel		808-245-2333

Central Līhu'e, just five minutes from the airport, and perfect for the budget-conscious traveler. 34 motel rooms, each furnished with two single beds, private baths, television and air-conditioning. On-site cafe, bakery and bar. *3173 Akāhi St., Līhu'e (FAX: 808-246-8988)*

CONDOMINIUMS and APARTMENTS

A more at-home atmosphere is available in self-contained apartments, and these are plentiful and very popular, particularly for vacationers and business travelers staying several weeks. Apartment sizes vary, as do amenities, furnishings and prices. The places listed here are in alphabetical order; there are many more units available through real estate and property management agents on Kaua'i. Many vacation rental apartments are individually owned, and several companies may represent the various owners in any given complex.

ACCOMMODATION

130

Alii Kai I & II	$$/$$$	I: 808-826-9921 II: 808-826-9988

Princeville complexes. Alii Kai I has 59 two-bedroom apartments, most with ocean views; Alii Kai II, on Hanalei Bluff, has 56 two-bedroom apartments, some with ocean views. Swimming pool, tennis and golf. *3830 Edward Road, Princeville*

Aston Kauai Beach Villas	$$-$$$$	800-922-7866 808-245-7711

A deluxe condominium complex situated outside of Līhu'e in a lovely landscaped garden setting complete with ponds and elegant swans, fronting the ocean. Studios (no air-conditioning) and spacious one- and two-bedroom suites (air-conditioned in bedrooms only) with full kitchens, private lanais and daily maid service. Four tennis courts (two are lighted), swimming pool, jet spa, barbecue grills and adjacent golf course (Wailua). Close to restaurants and shopping. *4330 Kaua'i Beach Drive, Līhu'e*

Banyon Harbor	$$/$$$	800-422-6926 808-245-7333

Near Kalapakī Beach. 248 two-bedroom units, with full kitchens, cable television, washer and dryer. Swimming pool, tennis court and shuffle board. Nearby golf courses (Kauai Lagoons, Wailua, Kiahuna), shops, restaurants and sandy swimming beach. *3411 Wilcox Rd., Līhu'e*

Cliffs at Princeville, The	$$$	800-622-6219 808-826-6219

Oceanfront Princeville complex. 194 units, many with ocean views, swimming pool, spa, golf, tennis and activities desk. *3811 Edward Rd.*

Embassy Suites Kauai	$$$$	800-8217-4427 808-826-6522

Princeville, at the Hanalei Bay Resort overlooking Hanalei Bay. 75 air-conditioned one-, two- and three-bedroom apartments, many with ocean views. Daily maid service. Golf, eight tennis courts, swimming pools, restaurant (Bali Hai), cocktail lounge (Happy Talk), shops, beauty salon, laundry facilities. *5380 Honoiki Rd., Princeville*

Garden Isle Cottages $$/$$$

Located in sunny Po'ipū. The Sea Cliff Cottages have studios, one- and two-bedroom units and are situated on a small ocean inlet where Waikomo Stream flows into the ocean overlooing Kōloa Landing. Hale Waipahu sits on the highest point in Po'ipū and overlooks Po'ipū Beach. Each of these units accommodates up to four guests, and has open-beamed ceilings, latticed dining lanai and an open tropical floor plan. Large studios also available. Tiled lap pool. Nearby shops, restaurants, golf and ocean activities. Office: *2666 Puuholo Rd., Kōloa*

Hale Moi $$

800-657-7751
808-826-9602

Princeville overlooking golf course. 40 apartments (studios, and one-and-one-half bedroom/two-bath suites), some with ocean view. Golf, tennis courts, health spa, pool and ocean activities are nearby. Units have complete kitchens, cable televisions, VCRs and private lanais. Restaurants, shopping nearby. This complex is currently being rebuilt after incurring damage in Hurricane Iniki, and scheduled to reopen in July of 1995. *5300 Ka Haku Road, Princeville*

Hanalei Colony Resort $$/$$$

800-628-3004
808-826-6235

A charming north shore resort located on 4.5 acres right on the beach at Hāena. 52 two-bedroom apartments, some overlooking the ocean. The resort is made up of 13 two-story buildings, each with four units. Apartments each have one bathroom, living room and dining area, private lanai and fully equipped kitchen. Swimming pool, Jacuzzi, barbecue and picnic areas, and laundromat. No televisions, stereos or telephones provided, as the focus is a restful environment. Charo's Restaurant next door. Nearby hiking areas and ocean activities. *5-7130 Kuhiō Hwy., Hāena*

Kaha Lani $$$/$$$$, W

800-922-7866
808-822-9331

East shore beachfront Aston property, 74 one-, two- and three-bedroom suites, with fully equipped kitchens, private lanais, and daily maid service. Swimming pool, lighted tennis court, jet-spa and barbecue grills. Next door to Lydgate State Park, with nearby golf (Wailua Golf Course) and shops. *4460 Nene Rd., Wailua*

Kapa'a Sands $$/$$$

800-222-4901
808-822-4901

Wailua oceanfront, 24 studio and two-bedroom apartments, swimming pool, beach, tennis, golf, shops, restaurant, lounge. *380 Papaloa Rd., Wailua*

Kapa'a Shore Resort $$/$$$

800-827-3922
808-822-3055

Oceanfront complex, 81 one- and two-bedroom apartments, partial air-conditioning, no room telephones, swimming pool, spa, and tennis. *4-0900 Kūhiō Hwy., Kapa'a*

ACCOMMODATION

131

Kauai Kailani I & II Apartments $ 808-822-3391

Centrally located in Kapa'a (KKI is on the ocean). 57 two-bedroom apartments, each with full kitchen. No phones in units; television and microwaves can be rented. TV room, Ping-Pong, shuffleboard and library, and both complexes have swimming pool. *856 Kūhiō Hwy., Kapa'a*

Kiahuna Plantation $$$/$$$$ 800-367-7052   808-742-6411

Po'ipū beachfront complex set on 35 lush acres, with lovely gardens, fruit trees, lagoon, lily ponds and tropical flowers. Its grounds were once part of the oldest sugar cane plantation in the state. 333 one- and two-bedroom apartments, each nicely furnished, featuring fully equipped kitchen, color TV/VCR, and ceiling fans. Daily maid service, laundry facilities, gas barbecues and picnic tables, activities desk, Hawaiana and children's programs, beach activities center, restaurant and two championship golf courses nearby. *2253 Po'ipū Road, Kōloa*

Kuhio Shores $$$ 800-367-8022   808-742-7555

Oceanfront at Po'ipū, 75 one- and two-bedroom apartments. This complex was reconstructed after incurring damage in Hurricane Iniki, and is scheduled to reopen for business in 1995. Close to golf, shopping, tennis and restaurants. *Po'ipū*

Lae Nani $$$/$$$$ 800-367-7052   808-822-4938

Operated by Colony Hotels and Resorts, this attractive Wailua beachfront complex has 70 one- and two-bedroom condominium units, with oceanfront, ocean, and garden views. Each offers a complete kitchen, color television and daily maid service. Large swimming pool and lighted tennis court. Walking distance from restaurants and numerous shops; minutes away from Wailua Golf Course. *410 Papaloa Rd., Kapa'a*

Mauna Kai Princeville $$/$$$ 808-826-6855

Princeville complex, with 46 two- and three-bedroom apartments, no ocean views, swimming pool, golf. *Hanalei*

Mokihana of Kauai $ 808-822-3971

Located oceanfront in Waipouli, this complex is for the budget-conscious. 79 studio apartments, each with refrigerator and hot plate in kitchen area. Microwave and blender can be rented. No phones in units. Recreation facilities include an 18-hole par 36 putting green, swimming pool, barbecue and picnic area, tennis court, shuffleboard and TV room. Complete laundry facilities. Site of the Bull Shed restaurant (see DINING). *796 Kūhiō Hwy., Waipouli*

Nihi Kai Villas $$$/$$$$, W   808-782-1412

Po'ipū complex, with 70 one-, two- and three-bedroom luxury low-rise apartments. Each unit has TV/VCR, fully equipped kitchen, washer and dryer. Near Brennecke Beach and one block from Po'ipū Beach Park. Ocean-front swimming pools, tennis courts, and barbecue areas. Two golf courses, restaurants and shopping close by. *1870 Hoone Rd., Po'ipū*

Pali Ke Kua at Princeville $$$ 800-535-0085
808-922-9700

Attractive low-rise Princeville condominium complex, cliffside setting. 98 one- and two-bedroom apartments, almost all with ocean views. Swimming pool, nearby golf and health spa, restaurant (Winds of Beamreach), whirlpool and private beach gazebo. Suites feature full kitchens, ceiling fans, washer/dryer and cable television. Lanais offer breathtaking mountain and ocean views. Operated by Marc Resorts Hawaii. *Princeville*

Plantation Hale $$$ 800-462-6262
808-822-4941

Coconut Plantation complex, 160 one-bedroom units. Air-conditioned, three swimming pools, beach, nearby shops and restaurants at adjacent Coconut Marketplace. *484 Kūhiō Hwy., Kapa'a*

Poipu Crater Resort $$/$$$ 800-367-8020
808-742-7400

Small Po'ipū complex, located in a crater (no view). 30 two-bedroom/two-bath units set on attractive grounds. Swimming pool, saunas, and tennis court. Close to golf, restaurants and shopping. *2330 Hoohu Rd., Po'ipū*

Poipu Kai Resort $$-$$$$, W   800-367-8020
808-742-7400

Attractive Po'ipū 110-acre beachfront property. 350 one- to four-bedroom units. Two beaches situated at either end of the property, Brennecke's and Shipwreck, and minutes away from Po'ipū Beach Park. All units include full kitchen, cable color television and HBO, washer/dryer, ceiling fans and private lanais. Six swimming pools, two Jacuzzis, restaurant (House of Seafood), lounge, large tennis center with nine courts and pro shop. Two 18-hole golf courses, ocean activities, shops and restaurants close by. Some gardenview units are wheelchair accessible. *2827 Po'ipū Rd., Po'ipū*

Poipu Kapili $$$/$$$$ 800-443-7714,
808-742-6449

At Po'ipū Beach, 60 one- and two-bedroom apartments, swimming pool, and tennis courts (lighted). Spacious rooms are equipped with television/VCR, stereo, ceiling fans and private lanais. *2221 Kapili Rd., Po'ipū*

		800-535-0085
Pono Kai Resort	$$$	808-922-9700

Kapa'a beachfront on 15 lush acres. 217 one- and two-bedroom units, mile-long beach, pool, jet-spa, sauna, two tennis courts, barbecue area and activities desk. Managed by Marc Resorts Hawaii. *1250 Kūhiō Hwy., Kapa'a*

		800-325-6423
Prince Kuhio	$-$$$, W	808-245-9337

Po'ipū complex adjacent to Prince Kūhiō Park, with good snorkeling bay and beach across the road (50 feet away). 62 studio, one-bedroom units and rooftop two-bedroom penthouses. All are complete with microwave ovens, full-size refrigerators, color cable television and lanais. Swimming pool, tropical gardens, guest laundry facilities, as well as barbecue grill and patio area. Beach House Restaurant (see DINING) across the street, and numerous other restaurants and shops nearby. *Po'ipū*

		800-535-0085
Pu'u Pō'ā	$$$/$$$$	808-922-9700

Princeville oceanfront bluff setting. 56 spacious two-bedroom condominiums, all with ocean view. Each unit is stylishly furnished and has two lanais, two baths, full kitchen, ceiling fans, washer/dryer, and cable television. Swimming pool, lighted tennis court, and secluded white sand beach. In close proximity to two excellent golf courses, health spa, shopping, restaurants and ocean activities. Managed by Marc Resorts Hawaii. *5454 Ka Haku Rd., Princeville*

Sealodge	$$/$$$	808-826-6751

Princeville oceanfront complex, 86 one- and two-bedroom apartments, almost all with ocean views, swimming pool, golf course. *Princeville*

		800-852-5317
Shearwater Resort	$$$/$$$$	808-826-6549

New cliff-top oceanview luxury villas at Princeville. Spacious two-bedroom condominiums (1260 sq. ft. of living area), each featuring designer furnishings, gourmet kitchen with decorator appliances, two master-size baths with private spas, 27-inch color television/VCR, stereo system and covered lanai. This is Pahio's newest resort, and was awarded the prestigious Gold Crown award in 1994 from Resort Condominium International. Secluded beach, championship golf courses, tennis courts, health spa, shops and restaurants nearby. *Princeville*

		800-827-6478
Sunset Kahili	$$/$$$	808-742-7434

Po'ipū oceanfront, 36 one- and two-bedroom apartments, all with ocean views. Units are equipped with full kitchens, microwaves, color cable television and washer/dryers. Swimming pool, sun deck, plumeria garden and recreation room. Close to Brennecke's Beach and Po'ipū Beach Park, restaurants, golf, tennis, health spas and shopping. *1763 Pe'e Rd., Po'ipū Beach*

| Waikomo Stream Villas | $$/$$$ | 808-325-5701 |
| | | 808-742-7220 |

Po'ipū resort property in lush tropical setting offering one- and two-bedroom units. Spacious garden-view apartments include gourmet kitchens, cable television/VCR and microwaves. Adult and children's pool, tennis, barbecue areas, and nearby beach. *2721 Po'ipu Rd., Po'ipū*

| Wailua Bay View | $$$ | 800-767-4707 |
| | | 808-245-4711 |

East shore oceanfront on Kaua'i's Coconut Coast, just ten minutes north of Līhu'e airport. 45 spacious one-bedroom apartments on Wailua Beach. Each unit is stylishly furnished, with private oceanfront lanai, full kitchen, cable television/VCR, and some have air-conditioned bedrooms. Swimming pool and white sand beach. *320 Papaloa Rd., Wailua*

| Whalers Cove | $$$$ | 800-367-7052 |
| | | 808-742-7571 |

Oceanfront at Po'ipū. 39 luxurious and elegantly decorated two-bedroom/two bath condominiums. Each unit has private lanai with sweeping ocean vistas, fully equipped kitchen, dining area, Jacuzzi tub in master bath, washer/dryer and daily maid service. Oceanside pool and spa. Close to golf, tennis, sandy beaches and shops. *2640 Puuholo Rd. Po'ipū*

A sunset walk along Po'ipū Beach.

BED & BREAKFAST HOMES & COTTAGES

There are a number of bed-and-breakfast (B&B) homes and cottages on Kaua'i available to visitors who want more cozy and intimate lodging than a hotel or condo might offer. Here we list, by area of the island and in alphabetical order, some of the B&B homes and cottages you may want to consider. Most have three-day minimum stays, and discounted rates for extended stays of a week or more. An asterisk (*) on a listing designates it as a Hawaii Visitors Bureau member.

At the end of this section is a listing of the local reservation services you may want to call to make your arrangements, if you prefer someone else to do the legwork for you. The advantage to using a reservation service is that it can save you time and money spent on long distance calls making your own arrangements, and the services are familiar with the various properties and can help you find just the right one to suit your budget and vacation needs.

A continental breakfast is included with your room (unless otherwise noted), normally consisting of toast, muffins or pastries, island fruits and/or juices. Many hosts add nice personal touches to make the morning meal a special experience.

EAST SHORE AREA B&B'S

Alohilani Bed & Breakfast Inn	$$, *	800-533-9316 808-823-0128

A lovely upcountry B&B in a quiet pastoral setting, with panoramic views of mountains, waterfalls and the ocean beyond. Charming detached cottage and several attractive, comfortable guestrooms in the main house, all stylishly decorated with lovely country antiques. A hot tub affords a wonderful view of lush greenery and the ocean beyond! Extra-special breakfasts are served on an open-air lanai or in a darling gazebo, with home-baked breads or muffins, fresh-squeezed juices and tropical jams made from fruits grown on the property. Hosts: Sharon Mitchell and William Whitney. Non-smoking guests only.

Candy's Cabin	$	808-822-5451

Located behind the mountain landmark, the Sleeping Giant, this is a 500-square-foot studio, offering peace and quiet, cool breezes and mountain views. Kitchenette and private entrance. Hostess: Candace Kepley.

House of Aleva	*	808-822-4606

Centrally located, directly across the street from 'Ōpaeka'a Waterfall, this B&B features three guestrooms with spacious shared bath. Breakfasts are customized to guests' particular health needs. Good choice for budget-minded. Hosts: Ernie and Anita Perry. Personal and travelers checks accepted, no credit cards. No children under ten years of age.

Kakalina's Bed & Breakfast $ 808-822-2328

This B&B offers "country comfort in a tropical setting". Situated on a lush three-acre flower farm in the foothills of Wai'ale'ale, with two guest units, one a spacious two-room unit with private entrance and sunning porch, the other a brand new studio with full kitchen. Breakfast includes fresh juice and fruit from the grounds. Just a five-minute drive to nearest beach. Hosts: Bob and Kathy Offley. Call collect for more information.

Kauai Calls Bed & Breakfast $/$$, * 808-822-9699

Nestled in the Wailua Valley between Sleeping Giant and Mt. Wai'ale'ale, near the Wailua River, Fern Grotto and Lydgate Park. Choice of studio apartment or guestroom. Hot tub available to guests and each room has recorded Hawaiian music, adding to the ambiance. Deluxe breakfasts. Caters to honeymooners. Host: Earle Schertell. Non-smokers only.

Kay Barker's Bed & Breakfast $ (& less)/$$, * 800-835-2845 808-822-3073

This B&B home is situated in a beautiful and quiet rural setting on the slopes of the Sleeping Giant. Four nicely furnished bedrooms in the main house, each with private bath, as well as a lovely, romantic Hibiscus Cottage, complete with wet bar, refrigerator, microwave and its own lanai, overlooking green pastures. Common areas include a spacious TV room, lanai area and extensive library. Free laundry service and generous continental breakfast. Host: Gordon Barker. Hawai'i resident discount of 20% when booked direct. Call from 7-11:00 a.m. Hawai'i time.

Keapana Center B & B $ (& less)/$$ 800-822-7968 808-822-7968

This tranquil retreat is set on three acres of rolling hills above Kapa'a. Nature lovers and new-agers will enjoy this peaceful environment. A number of simply, but comfortably furnished guestrooms are available, with either private or shared baths. A picturesque and spacious lounging area has attractive rattan furnishings and a relaxing hammock overlooking lush vegetation. There's also a one-bedroom cottage, as well as a yurt with its own kitchen, which is available on a weekly basis, with rustic outdoor shower and bathroom. A spacious Jacuzzi overlooks magnificent green mountain vistas. Groups of up to twenty (or so) can be accommodated, and are invited to make use of the enormous wooden-floored "great room" upstairs for meetings, lectures, healing work, etc. Good hiking and bike trails nearby; a five-minute drive to a safe sandy beach. A nurturing, non-smoking environment.

Lampy's Bed & Breakfast $ (& less), * 808-822-0478

Centrally located behind Sleeping Giant Mountain, close to Ōpaeka'a Falls and Wailua Bay. Small and cozy, this B&B's three guestrooms have private baths and private entrances, well-lit for late-night arrivals. Breakfast served in their garden gazebo. Hosts: Tom & Lampy Lowy.

ACCOMMODATION

Mohala Ke Ola $ 808-823-6398

This attractive and comfortable B&B retreat is in a peaceful neighborhood, surrounded by magnificent mountains, and set in the Wailua River Valley. The two guestrooms are bright and attractively furnished, each with private baths and entrances. A picturesque patio area has a breathtaking view of lush hillsides and a lovely waterfall, and is complete with a 25-foot swimming pool and relaxing Jacuzzi. A full range of body treatments, from massage to shiatsu, may be arranged. Guests have access to barbecue grill, microwave and refrigerator. Quiet, smoke-free environment. Nearest beaches are Wailua and Lydgate. Host: Ed Stumpf.

Mtn. View Manor Bed & Breakfast $, *   808-822-0406 / 808-822-4573

Set atop a mountain plateau, minutes away from nice beaches, mountain streams, hiking trails and golf courses. Beautiful view of Mt. Wai'ale'ale and waterfalls. Two suites available (one sleeps up to four, the other up to six), each with private baths and kitchenettes. A gazebo area has Jacuzzi and sauna for guests to enjoy. Hosts Jim and Jan Martin live in a separate residence on property, and can assist guests with activities and tours.

Rosewood Bed & Breakfast $ (& less)/$$, *   808-822-5216

A restored turn-of-the-century macadamia nut plantation house is the centerpiece of this picturesque B&B, located in the lush country pasturelands above Kapa'a. Two bright, stylishly-furnished guestrooms are located in the main house. The two-bedroom "Victorian Cottage", a smaller model of the main house, has lovely furnishings, oak floors throughout, with full kitchen, private bath, and outdoor shower. An intimate thatched-roof cottage, with kitchenette and private garden, is a relaxing retreat (no phone or TV) for the romantically-inclined. Budget-minded travelers or hikers will appreciate the very affordable "bunkhouse" rooms--clean, bright and cozy units, each with comfortable bunk beds, in-room sink, small refrigerator, toaster, coffee maker, hardwood floors, French windows and cathedral ceilings, and shared outdoor shower and bathroom. (Bunkhouse rates do not include breakfast, but breakfast may be purchased for a nominal additional cost). The grounds are beautifully landscaped, complete with a three-hole putting green. Smoke-free environment. Hosts: Rosemary and Norbert Smith.

Wailua Country Bed 'n Breakfast $/$$, *   808-822-0166

Tucked behind the Sleeping Giant mountain, this B&B has breathtaking mountain and waterfall views, situated on two acres with fruit trees, flowers and freshwater stream. Steps away from a park with tennis courts, hiking trails and swimming holes; other outdoor activities, shops and restaurants are nearby. Two suites (non-smoking) in the newly remodeled home have private master baths and mini-kitchens. Separate from the main residence is a luxury apartment, a large studio apartment, and two-bedroom cottage. Coffee, tea and fruit basket included; breakfast is an additional cost, served on request. Jacuzzi available for guests' use.

Winter's Mac Nut Farm & Inn $/$$, *,W   800-572-8156
800-822-3470

A tranquil country setting with beautiful mountain views, including Mt.
Wai'ale'ale, Sleeping Giant, waterfalls and surrounding green pastures. The
attractive main house has one guestroom with private bath, and a library and
screened lanais for guests' use. The nearby guest house is a lovely custom
built one-bedroom unit, with French doors, ceramic tile floors, full kitchen
and large private lanai with propane barbecue grill. (Note: guest house is
wheelchair accessible.) Generous breakfasts include home-grown fruit, and
homemade macadamia nut bread or muffins made with nuts grown on the
farm. Short drive to beaches, restaurants, shopping, and outdoor activities.
Hosts: Dale and Eileen Winters.

NORTH SHORE AREA B&B's

Bed, Breakfast & Beach at Hanalei Bay $/$$ (808) 826-6111

Conveniently situated in an attractive residential neighborhood, and just
150 yards from Hanalei Bay beach park (and a 15-minute drive from the
Kalalau Trail), this comfortable B&B offers a magnificent view of sunset from
its second floor lanai. Five stylishly-decorated guestrooms have private
baths and outdoor showers. Breakfast is served on the lanai and includes
smoothies, fresh fruit and homemade baked goods. Smoking outdoors only.
Hanalei River offers fun boating activities, and Hanalei Town has many cute
shops and restaurants. Proprietor: Carolyn Barnes.

Hale 'Aha Bed & Breakfast $$-$$$$, *   800-826-6733
808-826-6733

Located in the posh Princeville resort, this lovely upscale B&B is situated
on 1.5 acres fronting the Princeville Golf Course. Stylishly furnished in
pastel-hued Hawaiian decor, two guestrooms and two luxury suites are
available. The "crowning touch" is a 1000-square-foot luxury suite, occupy-
ing the entire top floor, a favorite of honeymooners. Suites are each furnished with Jacuzzi and kitchenette. A fabulous health spa is less than half a
mile away, and beaches, snorkeling and other outdoor activities can be
enjoyed nearby. Golf and tennis discounts available to guests. Rooms are
non-smoking. Fruit smoothies and Kona coffee are part of the extra-special
breakfast fare. Hosts: Herb and Ruth Bockelman.

Hale Ho'o Maha $, *   800-851-0291
808-828-1341

This spacious plantation-style home is situated near Kilauea on five
pastoral acres, just a few miles from Hanalei and Lumahai Beach. It offers
ocean, mountain and waterfall views. The house features koa wood floors,
marble baths and a large family room, with four guestrooms available. A full
gourmet kitchen is available for guests' use. Smoking and social drinking
acceptable. Hosts Toby and Kirby Searles are outdoors people. Toby, a
certified diver, offers to escort guests on underwater dives, if desired.

Kai Mana $$/$$$, *

800-837-1782
808-828-1280

Set atop a cliff and offering panoramic ocean and mountain views, this relaxing getaway is the paradise home of best-selling New Age author, Shakti Gawain *(Creative Visualization; Living in the Light)*. Four guestrooms are available, with private baths and entrances, as well as a charming one-bedroom cottage with a magnificent coastline view. A hot tub and spacious lanai are available for guests' enjoyment, and a cliffside trail leads to a lovely secluded beach. Massage and bodywork sessions may be arranged by appointment. "Serve yourself" continental breakfasts. Manager: Marilyn Draper.

North Country Farms $$ 808-828-1513

This picturesque B&B is a hand-built, one-bedroom redwood cottage in Kilauea, set on an organic fruit, vegetable and flower farm, and surrounded by thoroughbred and Arabian horse farms. One nice benefit for guests is the invitation to pick "as much as they can eat" of any of the fresh produce from the extensive garden to enjoy during their stay. The cottage can sleep up to four guests, and has a private bath and separate main room with living and dining areas, and kitchenette. A large deck has a small grill and outdoor shower. The nearest beach is a one-mile walk, and several beaches are less than five minutes away by car. Breakfast includes muffins, bagels, fruit, croissants, and more. The cottage is stocked with fruit bowl, coffee, juice and tea. Children welcome. Hosts: Lee Roversi and Chad Deal.

Tassa Hanalei $/$$, * 808-826-7298

This romantic and tranquil B&B was modeled after the well-known Buddhist retreat center in Big Sur, California, Tassajarra Hot Springs. The place looks and feels Hawaiian, is peaceful and relaxing, and is nestled in the last inhabitable valley before the spectacular Nā Pali Coast. Three richly decorated suites are available, each named for a member of the Hawaiian monarchy. The largest suite has a full kitchen and three sleeping areas, perfect for families, offering breathtaking views of waterfalls and Mt. Kamekeanu. A hot tub is available to guests, set next to cool river waters. Located close to snorkeling beaches, hiking trails and many other activities. Massage and bodywork sessions can be arranged for an extra charge. A delightful breakfast of beautifully arranged fruits and fresh baked goods is delivered to guest suites each morning. Family and group rates available. Proprietor: Ileah Van Hubbard.

SOUTH SHORE AREA B&B's

Gloria's Spouting Horn B&B $$$, *   808-742-6995

"Unmatched in cozy enchantment" is one of the many accolades given this intimate Po'ipū B&B, situated in a lovely spot just forty feet from the ocean, and a short distance from a safe swimming beach. The structure was totally rebuilt after the original one was destroyed in 1992's Hurricane Iniki. Three oceanfront guestrooms are available, each with private bath (featuring a deep Japanese-style soaking tub and separate shower stall), as well as an oceanfront lanai, wet bar and all the amenities. Hammocks are strung between coconut palms overlooking the beach, and there's even an outdoor lava rock beach shower (with hot water). Scenic Waimea Canyon and Hanalei Bay are within an hour's drive. Children under 14 not allowed; smoking permitted outside only. Hostess: Gloria Merkle.

Hale Honu at Po'ipū $$ 800-742-9619
                                            808-742-9618

Situated in sunny Po'ipū just half a block from the beach, with ocean and sunset views. The second floor guestroom has an ocean view and private bath. A living room area with open-beamed ceiling, a kitchen and large lanai are available for guests' use. Closest beach is "Keiki Beach", perfect for small children. Golf and tennis are a five-minute drive. Hyatt Regency nearby. Hostess: Carmela DeMarco.

Hale Kua $$ 808-332-8570

Situated on a hillside in Lāwai Valley, this B&B has panoramic ocean and mountain views. The peaceful setting is a developing tropical fruit and timber farm near Kōloa, and just a 15-minute drive from Līhu'e, Waimea Canyon, Po'ipu Beach and Salt Pond Beach. The guest cottage can sleep up to four, and has a kitchenette, television, and washer/dryer. Breakfast is optional, for a small additional fee. Hosts: Catherine and Bill Cowern.

Island Home, a B&B Inn $/$$, *   808-742-2839

Located in the beautifully landscaped Po'ipū Kai resort, this B&B has two tastefully decorated units, each with private bath and own entrance. Guests may enjoy the resort's swimming pool and Jacuzzi; tennis courts are a nominal fee; golf courses are nearby. Two beaches, Shipwreck and Po'ipū, are walking distance away. No smoking permitted in the house, and no children allowed. A large selection of videotapes and books is available to guests. Hosts Mike and Gail Beeson offer to help visitors with sight-seeing tours and other activities.

ACCOMMODATION

141

Poipu Bed & Breakfast Inn & Vacation Rentals	$$$, *	800-22-POIPU 800-552-0095 808-742-1146

This quaint romantic getaway in Po'ipū is a renovated 1933 plantation house with a huge Royal Poinciana "Flame Tree" in front. It has won awards from the Hawaii Visitors Bureau and the National Trust for Historic Preservation, as well as having been featured in many travel magazines. Beautifully furnished with wicker, pine antiques and carousel horses, each room has a luxurious private bath, most with a whirlpool tub. An airy sitting room has a nice library of books and videotapes for guests' free use. Delicious breakfasts are served on an open-air lanai. Condos and cottages from luxury oceanfront to budget are also offered (with rates ranging from $ to $$$$).

Seaview Suite Bed & Breakfast $/$$ 808-293-0070 (Oahu)

Located in quaint Kālaheo in a safe, upscale neighborhood, this B&B is situated in a lovely pastoral setting, surrounded by open meadows planted with banana and palm trees. The Seaview Suite is spacious enough to accommodate up to five guests, complete with full kitchen and extra-large bathroom. The Ti Room is a large studio, with kitchen, private lanai and nicely tiled bathroom. Each affords great ocean views, overlooking Po'ipū beaches, and includes a complimentary fruit basket and breakfast roll assortment. A barbecue grill is available to both units, on a lanai area. Discounts offered to senior citizens and Hawai'i residents, upon request. Special accommodations made for travelers with disabilities, and children are welcome. For reservations, call Linda Adams (on Oahu).

South Shore Vista $, *   808-332-9339

In the hillside community of Kālaheo, this bright, attractively furnished one-bedroom apartment is in a private home, with spectacular ocean and mountain views, just ten minutes away from good beaches and the Po'ipū Beach Resort. The unit includes a private bathroom, lovely well-stocked kitchenette, private lanai, and separate front and back entrances. Coffee, tea and oatmeal are provided for breakfast, or additional breakfast fare can be supplied for a nominal additional fee. A popular nine-hole golf course is nearby. Proprietress: Margy Parker.

Victoria Place $/$$, W, *   808-332-9300

Situated in the hills near Kōloa Town, in a quiet cul-de-sac overlooking lush jungle and cane fields. Three guestrooms are in one wing of the spacious house, each with private baths, and open directly through glass doors onto a swimming pool, with flowering walls of colorful and fragrant tropical blooms. A second-story lanai is available for guests to enjoy. The Shell Room is designed to accommodate disabled guests. A secluded studio apartment with private bath and own entrance is also available, ideal for honeymooners. Guests are pampered with a special poolside breakfast each morning. Hostess Edee Seymour was the recipient of the "Aloha Spirit" award in 1992, and is very helpful in directing her guests to the best beaches and restaurants, as well as assisting with rental cars and sight-seeing tours. *Country Inns Magazine* called Victoria's Place a "gourmet's delight".

B&B RESERVATION SERVICES

The following is a list of Hawai'i's bed-and-breakfast reservation services, which are knowledgeable about accommodations on each island, and can assist you in finding the right place to stay to fit your budget and traveling needs. If calling from the mainland, be aware of our time difference. Hawaiian Standard Time is five hours behind New York, four hours behind Chicago, three hours behind Denver and two hours behind San Francisco. Add an hour to these when Daylight Savings is in effect.

All Islands Bed & Breakfast	800-542-0344	808-263-2342
B&B Hawaiian Islands	800-258-7895	808-261-7895
Bed & Breakfast Hawaii, a Reservation Service Statewide	800-733-1632	808-822-7771
Bed & Breakfast Honolulu (Statewide)	800-288-4666	808-595-7533
Bed & Breakfast Pacific Hawaii	800-999-6026	808-486-8838
Bed & Breakfast Wailua Kauai, a Reservation Service Statewide	800-822-1176	808-822-1177
Hawaii's Best Bed & Breakfasts, a Reservation Service Statewide	800-262-9912	808-885-0550
Hawaiian Islands Bed & Breakfast & Vacation Rentals	800-258-7895	808-261-7895
Volcano Reservations Statewide Accommodations	800-736-7140	808-967-7244

An informative guidebook for bed-and-breakfast accommodations, entitled *Bed & Breakfast Goes Hawaiian* (278 pages), is published by Evie Warner and Al Davis, who operate **Bed & Breakfast Hawaii.** The book lists descriptions of B&B's throughout the islands, and includes thirty-two color photographs, as well as handy tips on sight-seeing activities, beaches and restaurants. The book is available through their office (1-800-733-1632) at a cost of $10. Another handy resource is an informative 25-page pamphlet published by Barbara and Susan Campbell of **Hawai'i's Best Bed & Breakfasts,** available free when booking reservations through their office at 1-800-262-9912.

VACATION RENTALS

There are literally hundreds of private homes and apartments on Kaua'i available as vacation rentals. Here we list only a few. There are many more which may be booked through vacation rental agents and property managers, some of which are noted below under "Vacation Rental Agents". The figure noted on each listing is the weekly rental rate , and rates are sometimes adjusted for extended stays.

Hale Kipa Golf Course Home	$1,300 *	**800-866-2539, 808-826-6657**

Located on the Princeville Golf Course, this private home has three master bedrooms, a full kitchen, swimming pool and tennis. Close to good restaurants, beaches, shopping, health spa and world class golf. Minimum stay is seven days, with maid service only on request. Golf packages are also available. Security deposit required.

Kahelelani	$1,950 *	**808-247-3637**

Private beachfront home at Hāena, on Kaua'i's north shore, with views of "Bali Hai" mountain, Hanalei Bay and the Nā Pali Coast. This architect-designed home sleeps twelve comfortably (the rate quoted above is for a maximum of six occupants), with three bedrooms, two full-size bathrooms and an outdoor shower. There's also a sleeping loft with two queen beds and separate bath. Amenities include beachfront spa, VCR/cable television, stereo and full laundry. Property manager : Gary Stice.

Waioli Vacation Rental	$575 *	**808-826-6405**

Situated in Hanalei, on Kaua'i's north shore, this unit is an 800-square-foot apartment in a private home, with the beach just 50 yards away. Quiet tropical setting with lovely mountain views. Accommodates two guests, and has one bedroom, full kitchen and bath, TV, stereo, laundry and other amenities. Proprietor Claudia Herfurt speaks fluent German.

VACATION RENTAL AGENTS

Kaua'i has more than two dozen property management agencies dealing with vacation rental units of various types and sizes. A selection of those with the widest range of properties is given here.

Anini Beach Vacation Rentals	800-448-6333	808-826-4000
Garden Island Rentals	800-247-5599	808-742-9537
Hanalei North Shore Properties	800-488-3336	808-826-9622
Kauai Paradise Vacations, Inc.	800-826-7782	808-826-7444
Kauai Vacation Rentals	800-367-5025	808-245-8841
Prosser Realty, Inc.	800-767-4707	808-245-4711
Vacation Homes of Kauai	800-325-5701	808-742-7220

COTTAGES

Another accommodation option on Kaua'i is to stay in your own private cottage. There are also several cottages listed under BED & BREAKFAST HOMES.

Classic Vacation Cottages $, *   808-332-9201

Located in the countryside of Kālaheo, these attractive self-contained cottages (four in all) have complete kitchens, carpeting, and feature antique stained leaded windows. Rates available with or without breakfast. Jacuzzi available, and daily linen service. Ten-minute drive to beaches, with nearby golf and tennis. Hosts: Richard and Wynnis Grow.

Koloa Landing Cottages $/$$, W   808-742-1470

Situated in sunny Po'ipū in a tropical garden setting, across the street from the ocean. The nearest beach is Po'ipū, a three-minute drive away. Five cottages and two studios (one has wheelchair access) accommodate from one to four guests, and each have full kitchens, showers, and good-size decks. There is also a two bedroom/two bath home with family room and dining area suitable for up to four guests. (A one-time clean-out fee is charged in addition to accommodation rates.) Coin-operated laundry facilities on site, as well as gas barbecue. Hosts: Hans and Sylvia Zeevat.

Royal Drive Cottages $/$$ 808-822-2321

Centrally located in a lush tropical setting on a secluded private drive in the hills above the Sleeping Giant mountain, with beaches, restaurants and shopping a short drive away. Individual tin-roofed cottages are cozy and comfortable, each with its own kitchenette. Host Bob Levine lives on-site in the main house and assists guests in planning their excursions.

Waimea Plantation Cottages $$$/$$$$, *
800-9-WAIMEA
808-338-1625

These historic former plantation workers' homes are examples of classic Hawai'i plantation architecture, and have been restored and updated with modern amenities and shady lanais. Situated in the seaside town of Waimea on an enormous oceanfront property, the grounds are beautifully land-scaped with tropical fruit trees and flowers, and graced with row upon row of swaying coconut palms. Cottages are each furnished with ceiling fans and period furniture of mahogany, koa and wicker. Large swimming pool and tennis court on property. In addition to the cottages, a 4000-square-foot five-bedroom "Manager's Estate" is available on a weekly basis, situated oceanfront. The Grove Dining Room restaurant is on property (see DIN-ING), its menu changing daily. A few other dining places are in nearby Hanapēpē. Spectacular sunset views, with the island of Ni'ihau visible in the distance. Good hiking trails in nearby Kōkee State Park. Close to Waimea Canyon, the "Grand Canyon of the Pacific".

Hāʻena Beach Park on the north shore has a camping facility.

CABINS and YOUTH HOSTEL

Adventurous souls with a taste for the outdoor life or traveling on a shoestring budget favor more rustic lodging. Tent camping is permitted in some parks on Kaua'i--a fun and economical option for families--and cabins are available at a few sites.

Kahili Mountain Park   *   808-742-9921

Centrally located just seven miles from Po'ipū, on 197 acres in the lush foothills of Kahili Mountain, twenty minutes from Līhu'e Airport. Behind the park, rising ridges with steep valleys create a dramatic backdrop. Ten rustic cabins sleep up to four people, with two larger cabins accommodating up to six; each has an inside half-bath, with an outdoor private shower, as well as a kitchen area. The most economical units are fifteen cabinettes, one-room cabins which can sleep up to five; guests share nearby bathrooms and showers with other guests. The new cabins are the "top of the line", able to accommodate up to four people, with full indoor bath/shower, kitchen area, and screened porch. All units are furnished, and linens, bedding, kitchen cookware and dishes, and bathroom supplies are included. Laundry on premises. Two hiking trails on property. Guests are asked to keep noise down between 8:00 p.m. and 8:00 a.m.

Kauai International Hostel

800-858-2295
808-823-6142

This low-budget dormitory-style hostel offers shared rooms for incredibly low prices, with private rooms also available. German, French and English spoken here. Located in the heart of Kapa'a, across from Kapa'a Beach. Transportation available to Nā Pali trails and other hiking areas.

Kōke'e Lodge   *   808-335-6061

Located in Kōke'e State Park, about a 90-minute drive from the Līhu'e Airport, this rustic lodge has a dozen cabins--two small one-room units and then two-bedroom units that sleep up to six or seven people--all furnished with stove, refrigerator, hot showers, basic eating and cooking utensils, bed linens, towels, blankets and pillows. Wood for the wood stoves is available for purchase. Restaurant serves a light breakfast as well as lunch (see DINING). Park rules apply, so maximum length of stay is five days. Write to Kōke'e Lodge at: P. O. Box 819, Waimea, Hawaii, 96796.

PRIVATE CAMPS

There are several private camps on Kaua'i you may want to contact for accommodations. They are listed here by location. Kōke'e area: **Kōke'e Methodist Camp** - 808-335-3429; **Kōke'e Hongwanji Camp** - 808-335-3444; **Camp Sloggett (YWCA)** - 808-245-5959 or 808-335-6060. Hā'ena (north shore): **Camp Naue Beach Camp (YMCA)** - 808-826-6419.

CAMPING: STATE PARKS

Permits are required for camping in state parks, and these may be obtained at the Division of State Parks' district office on Kaua'i at 3060 Eiwa Street, Room 306, Līhu'e, Hawaii 96766-1875 (808-241-3444), or write to P. O. Box 1671, Līhu'e, Hawaii 96766. It is best to get your permit as much in advance of your arrival as possible, as camping is popular in Hawai'i and campsites are in high demand during peak season (May to December).

There are no fees, but applications must include the number of persons for whom the permit is requested and their names. Camping is limited to five days in any thirty-day period.

State parks where camping is permitted are: **Kōke'e State Park** (central mountains--four areas, Waimea and Koai'e Canyons--five areas); **Polihale State Park** (west coast); **Lydgate State Park** (east coast) and **Nā Pali Coast State Park** (north coast) in the Hanakāpī'ai, Hanakoa and Kalalau Valleys.

CAMPING: COUNTY BEACH PARKS

Kaua'i County camping permits are issued for four days at a time and are renewable for four days; there is a charge of $3.00 per person per night, and requests must include the number of persons for whom the permit is to be issued, along with their names and ages.

Reservations may be made by mail (Division of Parks and Recreation, 4193-A Hardy Street, Bldg. 5, Līhu'e, Hawaii, 96766), but permits must be picked up in person at the address included with your verification.

A map of the parks, available at the Department, lists the following camping areas: **Lucy Wright Beach Park,** Waimea; **Salt Pond Beach Park,** Hanapēpē; **Niumalu Beach Park,** Niumalu (on the Hule'ia River just upstream from Nāwiliwili Harbor); **Hanamā'ulu Beach Park,** Hanamāulu; **Anahola Beach Park,** Anahola; **'Anini Beach Park,** Anahola; and **Hā'ena Beach Park,** Hā'ena. All parks have restroom facilities and showers.

148

✻ designates listing as member of Hawaii Visitors Bureau

ET CETERA

Other Services
Island Weddings
Traveling with Children
Travelers with Disabilities
Other Islands

OTHER SERVICES

H ere we cover a miscellany of other services that did not lend themselves to appropriate inclusion in other sections of the guidebook--some things you just might need along the way, from dry cleaning to having a letter typed and faxed to your office back home.

LAUNDRY and DRY CLEANING

The need for a laundromat can be urgent, especially for hikers and campers. These are found in Līhu'e at **Kapaa Laundry Center** (1105-J Kūhiō Hwy, Kapa'a - 822-3113), and in Hanamāulu at **Plaza Laundry** (246-9057).

Laundry and dry cleaning service in south shore areas is available through **Up-To-Date Cleaners** at several locations (Līhu'e - 245-6621, Kōloa - 742-1628, Waimea - 338-1032); they also offer pickup and delivery service at Princeville Center (826-7331).

Some hotels will also handle this service for guests.

LUGGAGE and SHOE REPAIR

The Shoe Repair Shop in Kukui Grove Center (245-6543) in Līhu'e town services the leatherwork needs of the whole island.

LIBRARIES

Kaua'i's libraries offer lending rights to visitors who obtain a local library card during their stay. Branches of the **Kaua'i Regional Library** are located in Kapa'a (822-5041), Līhu'e (245-3617), Kōloa (742-1635), Hanapēpē (335-5811) and Waimea (338-1738).

BUSINESS SERVICES

Increasingly, business visitors in particular have need of secretarial and other executive services while in the islands.

Mailbox of Kaua'i in Kapa'a (822-1667) provides typing, fax and copy services, as well as UPS and Federal Express. In Princeville, **Ruthie's Secretarial Services** (826-7750) offers a full range of office services.

In Hanapēpē, **Sharon's Office Service** (335-0066) offers word processing, secretarial and notarial services, as does **Kīlauea Secretarial and Notary Service** in Kīlauea (828-1948).

Popular among visitors is the celebrated event of getting married or renewing vows. Numerous enterprises are engaged in the business of making people's romantic dreams of getting married in a tropical setting come true. So many spots are splendidly suited to the purpose that the difficulty is in choosing.

The most popular wedding site is the Fern Grotto on the Wailua River; **Smith's Motor Boat Service** can make arrangements. There are also, of course, many lovely indoor settings, but outdoor ceremonies are overwhelmingly preferred. Some hotels have special wedding consultants on their staffs. The **Kauai**

Marriott has a lovely Chapel by the Sea at Kauai Lagoons, with breathtaking views of nearby Kalapaki Bay. Couples are transported to the ceremony by a white horse-drawn bridal carriage. The Marriott's wedding coordinator (808-241-6021) can help with all of the arrangements.

There are also companies that arrange or assist with every detail of wedding ceremonies and celebrations. Kaua'i's wedding specialists are listed in the Kaua'i Yellow Pages under "Wedding". Many seek outdoor settings off the beaten wedding path, and offer couples special romantic touches for their special occasion.

ET CETERA

151

Many couples choose a natural open-air setting as a wedding site on Kaua'i.

POST OFFICES

Last but not least is your friendly neighborhood post office. Post office hours are Mon.-Fri. 8:00 a.m.-4:30 p.m., Sat. 8:00 a.m.-12:00 noon. Most post offices are located on the main highway. They are located at:

Anahola	(822-4710)	96703
Kekaha	(337-1322)	96752
'Ele'ele	(335-5338)	96705
Kīlauea	(828-1721)	96754
Hanalei	(826-6471)	96714
Kōloa	(742-6565)	96756
Hanamā'ulu	(245-3851)	96715
Lāwa'i	(332-9161)	96765
Hanapēpē	(335-5433)	96716
Līhu'e	(246-0793)	96766
Kalāheo	(332-8583)	96741
Makaweli	(338-9921)	96769
Kapa'a	(822-5421)	96746
Puhi	(246-8636)	96766
Kaumakani	(335-3641)	96747
Waimea	(338-9973)	96796
Keālia	(822-3181)	96751

TRAVELING WITH CHILDREN

Kaua'i is an ideal destination for family vacations. The island's relaxed, easy-going life-style, boundless outdoor activities and wholesome local entertainment provide children (and parents) with a variety of diversions.

Some hotels offer daily programs for children, such as the Hyatt Regency's "Camp Hyatt". These might include hula lessons, lei making and building sand castles.

In this outdoor-oriented vacation land, visits to the seashore top the list of possible family outings. The appropriateness of Kaua'i's beaches for family excursions has been thoroughly researched by frequent visitor Lenore Horowitz, and her descriptions, of great value to

Early signs of the surfer syndrome

parents, are noted in her book, *Kauai Underground Guide*. She also relates experiences she and her family have had with numerous restaurants on the island. For travelers with children, this book is recommended.

TRAVELERS WITH DISABILITIES

There are a limited special facilities for persons with disabilities on Kaua'i. We have previously noted those restaurants and accommodations accessible to guests in wheelchairs, with the letter "W" in the heading.

TRANSPORTATION

Special transportation on Kaua'i is limited, all vans with lifts being assigned to specific program services. Hand controls for cars can be arranged with 24-hour advance notice through Avis, Alamo, Hertz, Budget and Dollar rental car agencies. Permits for parking in restricted access zones are available from the Police Station (3060 'Umi Street, Līhu'e, Hawai'i 96766) with a doctor's certification or a parking permit from the applicant's place of residence. For information on special transportation needs, visitors may call 241-6420 or contact the State Commission on Persons with Disabilities (808-241-3308 - voice/TDD). Additionally, Akita Enterprises (245-5344) has vans with lifts which can accommodate those in wheelchairs, available for sight-seeing excursions (8:00 a.m. to 1:00 p.m.) at a rate of $48/hour (two-hour minimum).

SUPPORT SERVICES

Personal care attendants, personal companions, health aides, nurse aides and voluntary companions during visits to Kaua'i are available through Kauai Center for Independent Living (808-245-4034), G. N. Wilcox Memorial Hospital (808-245-1100 x 2248). For travelers older than sixty-two, the Office of Elderly Affairs (808-241-6400) can provide assistance.

MEDICAL EQUIPMENT

Supplies such as wheelchairs, walkers, canes and crutches are available for sale or rent from Kuhio Home Health (822-0927), and AB Medical (245-4995).

PHYSICIANS

The Kauai Medical Group at Wilcox Hospital (245-1500 or 245-1831 after hours) provides twenty-four-hour on-call physician referral service, with clinics located in north, east, and south shore areas. The Wilcox Medical Clinic in Waimea (338-1645), Kōloa/Po'ipū (742-1677) and Līhu'e (246-6900) is another option, open Monday through Friday from 9:00 a.m. to 4:30 p.m. and Saturdays from 9:00 to 11:30 a.m. Their after-hours and emergency telephone number is 338-9431. Another referral service is **Health Link** (245-1002) opens Monday to Friday.

OTHER ISLANDS

Each of the main Hawaiian islands has its own special magic, and *The Essential Guide to O'ahu, The Essential Guide to Maui* and *The Essential Guide to Hawai'i, the Big Island* provide the same in-depth coverage of those islands as does this guidebook. We hope you can visit all of our islands and discover for yourself the unique charm--past and present--of each.

Just over seventeen miles west of Kaua'i, across the Kaulakahi Channel, is the small, privately owned island of **Ni'ihau.** Except for short helicopter tours, access to this island has been restricted to residents for well over a century. Lying sixty-three miles south of Kaua'i, across the Ka'ie'ie Channel, is the heavily populated island of **O'ahu,** the capital of the state of Hawai'i. The island of **Moloka'i,** mellow and uncrowded, lies nearly twenty-six miles across the Kaiwi Channel from O'ahu.

Only nine miles from Moloka'i, across the Kalohi Channel, is **Lāna'i,** mostly owned by Castle and Cook and planted with pineapples. The quaint Hotel Lanai (808-565-4700), a traditional Hawaiian style hotel built in the 1920s, operates in Lāna'i City. The elegant Lodge at Koele (800-223-7637 or 808-565-3800) is situated on twenty-one acres in the highlands skirting Lāna'i City, and the lovely Manele Bay Hotel (800-624-8849 or 808-565-3800) sits beachfront on the south shore, with breathtaking views of Hulopoe Bay and the island of Maui. These last two hotels, the island's newest, offer visitors luxurious accommodations in spectacular surroundings. The island is a golfers' paradise, as well, with three challenging courses.

The not-quite-nine-mile Pailolo Channel separates Moloka'i from **Maui.** The island's motto 'Maui nō ka oi' means 'Maui is the best'. Tiny **Kaho'olawe,** not quite seven miles off the southern coast of Maui, was used, until recently, by the military as a target for bombing practice, and any landing on the island was prohibited by law. Today, the island has been returned to the state and is no longer being bombed, however, due to the danger of live ammunition shells present on the island, it is not accessible to visitors.

Nearly thirty miles southeast of Maui, across the 'Alenuihāhā Channel, is the island of **Hawai'i** commonly referred to as **'the Big Island'.** Youngest in the island chain, its active volcano, Kīlauea, is still building the coastline.

Hawaiians as well as visitors travel amongst our islands often, and the high volume of traffic makes interisland air transportation economical and efficient. Flights are short, the longest taking around half an hour. Many interisland flights connect in Honolulu, but some fly directly between islands other than O'ahu. Aloha, Aloha Island Air, Hawaiian, and Mahalo are the main interisland carriers. American Airlines also has interisland flights as extensions of its inbound and outbound flights via Honolulu. Air Molokai offers service between Moloka'i and the neighbor islands of Maui, Lāna'i and O'ahu. An interisland ferry also transports passengers traveling between Maui and Moloka'i.

APPENDIX

Address & Phone Numbers
Word Lists
Recommended Reading
Index

VEHICLE RENTALS

AUTOMOBILES

Alamo Rent A Car	Lihu'e Airport	246-0645
		Toll-free 800-327-9633
Avis Rent A Car	Lihu'e Airport	245-3512
	Princeville Airport	826-9773
	Hyatt Regency	742-1627
		Toll-free 800-321-3712
Budget Rent A Car	Lihu'e Airport	245-1901
		Toll-free 800-527-0700
Dollar Rent A Car	Lihu'e Airport	245-3651
		Toll-free 800-800-4000
Hertz Rent A Car	Lihu'e Airport	245-3356
	Princeville Airport	826-7455
		Toll-free 800-654-3131
National Car Rental	Lihu'e Airport	245-5636
		Toll-free 800-227-7368
Westside U-drive	Po'ipū	332-8644

BICYCLES

Bicycle John	3142 Kūhiō Hwy., Lihu'e	245-7579
" "	4504 Kukui, Kapa'a	822-3495
Bicycles Kauai	1379 Kūhiō Hwy., Kapa'a	822-3315
Kayak Kauai Outfitters	4-1340 Kūhiō Hwy., Kapa'a	822-0577
Outfitters Kauai	2827-A Po'ipū Rd., Po'ipū	742-9667
Pedal & Paddle	Ching Young Village, Hanalei	826-9069
" "	Kauai Village, Kapa'a	822-2005

LIMOUSINE SERVICE

Custom Limo	246-6318
North Shore Limo	826-6189

MOPEDS

Honda Two Wheels	4555 Pouli Rd., Kapa'a	822-7283
Pedal & Paddle	Ching Young Village, Hanalei	826-9069
" "	Kauai Village, Kapa'a	822-2005

TAXICAB SERVICE

ABC Taxi of Kauai	822-7641
Aloha Taxi	245-4609
Al's VIP Airport Stretch Limo Taxis	742-1390
Hanamaulu Taxi	245-3727
Kauai Cab Service	246-9554
Lorenzo's Taxi Service	245-6331
North Shore Cab & Tours	826-6189
Scotty Taxi	245-7888

WATER SPORTS:
EQUIPMENT & INSTRUCTION

SCUBA DIVING

Aquatic Adventures	4-1380 Kūhiō Hwy., Kapa'a	822-1434
Bay Island Water Sports	Princeville Hotel	826-7509
Bubbles Below	6251 Hauaala Rd., Kapa'a	822-3483
Dive Kauai	4-976 Kūhiō Hwy., Kapa'a	822-0452
Fathom Five Adventures	3450 Po'ipū Rd., Po'ipū	742-6991
Nitrox Tropical Divers	Kapa'a	822-7333
Ocean Odyssey	4331 Kauai Beach Dr., Waipouli	245-8681
Seasport Divers	2827 Po'ipū Dr., Po'ipū	742-9303
SNUBA Tours of Kauai		823-8912
Wet 'n Wonderful	Kapa'a	742-7959

SNORKELNG

Fathom Five Adventures	3450 Po'ipū Rd.	742-6991
Kauai Snorkel Rental	Coconut Marketplace	823-8300
Pedal & Paddle	Ching Young Village, Hanalei	826-9069
" "	Kauai Village, Kapa'a	822-2005
Snorkel Bob's	4480 Ahukini Rd., Līhu'e	245-9433
" "	Po'ipū	742-8322

SURFING & BODY BOARDING

Aquatic Adventures	4-1380 Kūhiō Hwy., Kapa'a	822-1434
Dive Kauai	4-976 Kūhiō Hwy., Kapa'a	822-0452
Fathom Five Adventures	3450 Po'ipū Rd., Po'ipū	742-6991
Hanalei Surf Company	5-5161 Kūhiō Hwy., Hanalei	826-9000
Kauai Water Ski and Surf	4-356 Kūhiō Hwy., Kapa'a	822-3574
Oberg, Margo	(instruction)	742-1750
Progressive Expressions	5428 Kōloa Rd., Po'ipū	742-6041

WATER SKIING

Kauai Water Ski & Surf Co.	4-356 Kūhiō Hwy., Kapa'a	822-3574

WIND SURFING

'Anini Beach Windsurfing	Hanalei	826-9463
Hanalei Sailboards	5-5161 Kūhiō Hwy., Hanalei	826-9000
Harvel, Celeste *(instruction)*	Hanalei	828-6838

BOATING & WATER TOURS

INTERISLAND CRUISES

American Hawaii Cruises	800-765-7000

KAYAKING, CANOEING

Hanalei Surf Co.	5-5161 Kūhiō Hwy., Hanalei	826-9000
Island Adventure	Līhu'e	
Kauai Water Ski & Surf Co.	4-356 Kūhiō Hwy., Kapa'a	822-3574
Kayak Kauai Outfitters	Hanalei	826-9844
Paradise River Rentals	Kilohana Plantation	245-9580
Pedal & Paddle	Ching Young Village, Hanalei	826-9069
" "	Kauai Village, Kapa'a	822-2005
The Fun Lady	4-746 Kūhiō Hwy., Waipouli	822-7447

WATER TOURS

Capt. Andy's Sailing Adventure	822-7833
Captain Zodiac Raft Expeditions	826-9371
Gent-Lee Fishing and Sightseeing Charters	245-7504
Hanalei Sea Tours	826-7724
Hawaii Rafting Expiditions	335-9909
Kauai River Adventure	245-9662
Lady Ann Cruises	335-9909
Liko Kauai Cruises	338-0333
Nā Pali Adventures	826-6804
Smith's Motor Boat Service	822-5213
Wai'ale'ale Boat Tours	822-4908

GUIDED LAND TOURS

Akita Enterprises	245-5344
Gray Line-Kauai	245-3344
Kauai Downhill *(bicycling)*	245-1774
Kauai Island Tours	245-4777
Kauai Mountain Tours	245-7224
North Shore Cab & Tours	245-4777
Trans Hawaiian Kauai	245-5108

HELICOPTER TOURS

Air Kauai Helicopter Tours	246-4666
Jack Harter Helicopters	245-3774
Niihau Helicopter Inc.	335-3500
Ohana Helicopter Tours	245-3996
Papillon Hawaiian Helicopters	826-5691
Safari Helicopters	246-0136
South Sea Tours & Helicopters	245-2222
Will Squyres Helicopter Service	245-7541

SPORTING ACTIVITIES

BICYCLING

Bicycle John	3142 Kūhiō Hwy., Līhu'e	245-7579
	4504 Kukui, Kapa'a	822-3495
Bicycles Kauai	1379 Kūhiō Hwy., Kapa'a	822-3315
Kauai Downhill	Līhu'e	245-1774
Kayak Kauai Outfitters	Po'ipū	822-0577
Outfitters Kauai	Kōloa	742-9667
Pedal & Paddle	Ching Young Village, Hanalei	826-9069
Pedal & Paddle	Kauai Village, Kapa'a	822-2005

FISHING

'Anini Fishing Charters (Sea Breeze IV)	828-1285
Gent-Lee Fishing and Sightseeing Charters	245-7504
Liko Kauai Cruises	338-0333
Sea Lure	822-5963
Sport Fishing Kauai	742-7013
True Blue Charters	246-6333

FITNESS CENTERS & SPAS

Anara Spa	Hyatt Regency Kauai	742-1234
Hamer Hed Fitness	Kauai Village, Kapa'a	823-6334
Kauai Athletic Club	Kukui Grove Center, Līhu'e	245-5381
Prince Health Club & Spa	Princeville	826-5030

GOLF

Kauai Lagoons Golf & Racquet Club	241-6000
Kiahuna Golf Club	742-9595
Kukuiolono Golf Course	332-9151
Poipu Bay Resort Golf Course	742-8711
Princeville Resort	826-5004
Wailua Golf Course	241-6666

HIKING

Dept. of Land & Natural Resources (Forestry & Wildlife Div.) 587-0166
Sierra Club (O'ahu) 538-6616

HORSEBACK RIDING

CJM Country Stables Po'ipū 742-6096
Garden Island Ranch Kikiaola Beach 338-0052
Pooku Stables Hanalei 826-6777

HUNTING

Div. of Conservation and Resources Enforcement (O'ahu) 587-0077
Div. of Forestry & Wildlife 241-3433
Hunting Seasons Hotline 587-0171

KITE FLYING

High Performance Kites Ala Moana Ctr. (O'ahu) 947-7097
Kauai Kite & Hobby Princeville Center 826-9144
Kite Fantasy Kaimana Beach (O'ahu) 922-5483
Paradise River Rentals Kilohana Plantation 245-9580

TENNIS

Kaua'i County Dept. of Recreation 241-6660
Kauai Lagoons Golf
  & Racquet Club Līhu'e 241-6000
Kiahuna Tennis Club Po'ipū 742-9533
Princeville Tennis Center Princeville 826-3620

RESTAURANTS

EAST SHORE AREA

A Pacific Cafe Kauai Village, Kapa'a 822-0013
Barbecue Inn 2982 Kress St., Līhu'e 245-2921
Bull Shed 796 Kūhiō Hwy., Waipouli 822-3791
Cafe Portofino 3501 Rice St., Līhu'e 245-2121
Dragon Inn Chinese Rest. Waipouli Plaza, Waipouli 822-3788
Flying Lobster Kauai Coconut Beach Resort 822-3455
Gaylord's Restaurant Kilohana Plantation 245-9593
Hamura Saimin Stand 2956 Kress St., Līhu'e 245-3271
Hanamāulu Restaurant
  & Tea House Hwy. 56, Hanamā'ulu 245-2511
JJ's Broiler Anchor Cove Ctr., Nāwiliwili 246-4422
Jacaranda Terrace Outrigger Kauai Beach, Līh'ue 245-1955
Jolly Roger Restaurant Waipouli 822-3451

160

Kapa'a Fish & Chowder House	1639 Kūhiō Hwy., Kapa'a	822-7488
Kauai Chop Suey	3501 Rice St., Līhu'e	245-8790
Kiibo Rest. & Sushi Bar	2991 Umi St., Līhu'e	245-2650
King and I Thai Cuisine	4-901 Kūhiō Hwy., Kapa'a	822-1642
Kintaro Japanese Steak House	4-370 Kūhiō Hwy., Kapa'a	822-3341
Kountry Kitchen	1485 Kūhiō Hwy., Kapa'a	822-3511
Mema Cuisine	361 Kūhiō Hwy., Kapa'a	823-0899
Norberto's El Cafe	4-1373 Kūhiō Hwy., Kapa'a	822-3362
Ono Family Restaurant	4-1292 Kūhiō Hwy., Kapa'a	822-1710
Papaya's Garden Cafe	Kauai Village, Kapa'a	823-0190
The Planter's Restaurant	Hwy. 56, Hanamā'ulu	245-1606
The Tip Top Motel Cafe	3173 Akahi St., Līhu'e	245-2333
Tokyo Lobby	3501 Rice St., Līhu'e	245-8989
Voyage Room	Kauai Coconut Beach Resort	822-3455
Wailua Marina Rest.	Hwy. 56, Wailua	822-4311
Waipouli Deli & Rest.	Waipouli Town Center, Kapa'a	822-9311

SOUTH SHORE AREA

Beach House	5022 Lāwai Rd., Kōloa	742-1424
Brennecke's Beach Broiler	Ho'one Rd., Po'ipū	742-7588
Brick Oven Pizza	2-2555 Kaumuali'i Hwy., Kalāheo	332-8561
Camp House Grill	Hwy. 50, Kalāheo	332-9755
Dondero's	Hyatt Regency Kauai, Kōloa	742-1234
The House of Seafood	1941 Po'ipū Rd., Po'ipū	742-6433
Ilima Terrace	Hyatt Regency Kauai, Kōloa	742-1234
Kalaheo Steak House	4444 Papalina Rd., Kalāheo	332-9780
Keoki's Paradise	Po'ipū Shopping Village, Po'ipū	742-7534
The Koloa Broiler	Old Kōloa Town	742-9122
Roy's Poipu Bar & Grill	Po'ipū Shopping Village, Po'ipū	742-5000
Taqueria Nortenos	2827-A Po'ipū Rd., Po'ipu	742-7222
Tidepools	Hyatt Regency Kauai, Kōloa	742-1234

SOUTHWEST SHORE AREA

The Espresso Bar	3830 Hanapēpē Rd., Hanapēpē	335-8544
Green Garden	13949 Kaumuali'i Hwy., Hanapēpē	335-5422
The Grove Dining Room	9400 Kaumuali'i Hwy., Waimea	338-2300
Kōkee Lodge	3600 Kōke'e Rd., above Waimea	335-6061

NORTH SHORE AREA

Bali Hai Restaurant	Hanalei Bay Resort, Princeville	826-6522
Black Pot Luau Hut	Aku Rd., Hanalei	826-9871
Cafe Hanalei and Terrace	Princeville Hotel	826-9644
Casa di Amici	2484 Keneke St., Kīlauea	828-1388
Charo's Restaurant & Bar	5-7132 Kūhiō Hwy., Hāena	826-6422

NORTH SHORE AREA (Continued)

Chuck's Steak House	Princeville Shopping Center	826-6211
Hanalei Dolphin Restaurant and Fish Market	Hwy. 56, Hanalei	826-6113
The Hanalei Gourmet	5-5161 Kūhiō Hwy., Hanalei	826-2524
La Cascata Restaurant	Princeville Hotel	826-2761
Tahiti Nui	Hwy. 56, Hanalei	826-6277
Tropical Taco	Hanalei	826-6878
Winds of Beamreach	Pali Ke Kua Resort, Princeville	826-6143

LU'AU

Kauai Coconut Beach Resort	Coconut Plantation, Kapa'a	822-3455
Smith's Tropical Paradise	Marina State Park, Wailua	822-4654
Tahiti Nui	Kūhiō Hwy., Hanalei	826-6277

FAST FOODS

Brick Oven Pizza	2-2555 Kaumuali'i Hwy., Kalāheo	332-8561
Bubba's Burgers	Kapa'a	823-0069
	Hanalei	826-7839
Burger King	Kapa'a Shopping Ctr.	822-2083
	4440 Kukui Grove , Līh'ue	245-5335
Dairy Queen	4302 Rice St., Līhu'e	245-2141
	Eleele Center, Eleele	335-5293
	Waimea	338-1911
Domino's Pizza	3100 Kūhiō Hwy., Līhu'e	246-0303
Duane's Ono Char Burger	Anahola	822-9181
Hamura Saimin Stand	2956 Kress St., Līhu'e	245-3271
Jack in the Box	3160 Kūhiō Hwy., Līhu'e	246-4432
Kentucky Fried Chicken	3229 Kūhiō Hwy., Līhu'e	245-4993
	4-919 Kūhiō Hwy., Kapa'a	823-0381
McDonald's	3-3113 Kūhiō Hwy., Līhu'e	245-6123
	4-0771 Kūhiō Hwy., Kapa'a	822-7290
Mustard's Last Stand	corner Kōloa Rd. at Hwy. 50	332-7245
Papaya's Garden Cafe	Kauai Village, Kapa'a	823-0190
Paradise Pizza	Kauai Village, Kapa'a	823-8253
Pau Hana Pizza	Kong Lung Center, Kīlauea	828-2020
Pizza Hut	3-3171 Kūhiō Hwy., Līhu'e	245-9531
	Waipouli Town Center, Kapa'a	822-7433
Sizzler	4361 Kūhiō Hwy., Kapa'a	822-7404
Taco Bell	4422 Kukui Grove, Līhu'e	245-9633
	4-927 Kūhiō Hwy., Kapa'a	822-1919
The Hanalei Gourmet	5-5161 Kūhiō Hwy., Hanalei	826-2524
Tropical Taco	Hanalei	826-6878
Waipouli Deli & Rest.	Waipouli Town Center, Kapa'a	822-9311

BAKERIES

Garden Isle Bake Shop	3501 Rice St., Līhu'e	245-6070
Green Garden	13749 Kaumuali'i Hwy., Hanapēpē	335-5422
Kauai Kitchens	Kōloa	742-1712
	Rice Shopping Center, Līhu'e	245-4513
	Waimea	338-1315
Kīlauea Bakery	Kīlauea	828-2020
Omoide Bakery& Deli	Hanapēpē	335-5291
Tip Top Bakery	3173 Akāhi, Līhu'e	245-2333
Village Snack & Bake Shop	Ching Young Villace, Hanalei	826-6841

SWEETS

Baskin Robbins	3-3122 Kūhiō Hwy., Līhu'e	246-1131
Dairy Queen	4302 Rice St., Līhu'e	245-2141
	Eleele Center, Eleele	335-5293
	Waimea	338-1911
Lappert's Ice Cream	Coconut Marketplace, Kapa'a	822-0744
	1-3555 Kaumuali'i Hwy., Hanapēpē	335-6121
	Kōloa	742-1272
	Princeville Center	826-7393
Popo's Cookies	971-E Kūhiō Hwy., Kapa'a	822-6911
TCBY Yogurt	4-361 Kūhiō Hwy., Līhu'e	822-7077
Zack's Famous Frozen	Kukui Grove Center, Līhu'e	246-2415
Yogurt and Cafe	Coconut Marketplace	822-2112

COCKTAIL LOUNGES & NIGHT SPOTS

Captains	Hyatt Regency Kauai, Kōloa	742-1234
Gilligan's	Outrigger Kauai Beach Hotel	245-1955
Kuhio's Nightclub	Hyatt Regency Kauai, Kōloa	742-1234
Legends Nightclub	Nāwiliwili	246-0491
Seaview Lounge	Hyatt Regency Kauai, Kōloa	742-1234
Stevenson's Library	Hyatt Regency Kauai, Kōloa	742-1234
The Happy Talk Lounge	Hanalei Bay Resort, Hanalei	826-6522
The Jolly Roger	Waipouli	822-3451
The Living Room	Princeville Hotel	826-9644
The Lobby Lounge	Outrigger Kauai Beach Hotel	245-1955

ESPRESSO BARS

Kalāheo Coffee Co. & Cafe	Kalāheo	332-5858
Old Hanalei Coffee Co.	Hanalei Center	826-6717
Papaya's Garden Cafe	Kauai Village, Kapa'a	823-0190
The Espresso Bar	3830 Hanapēpē Rd., Hanapēpē	335-5011

SHOPS

8 Bells	2-2514 Kaumuali'i Hwy., Kalāheo	332-7022
A Romantic Rose	4-1302 Kūhiō Hwy., Kapa'a	822-4781
Artists Gallery of Kauai	Ching Young Village, Hanalei	826-6441
Bamboo Silks	Kūhiō Hwy., Hanalei	826-1811
Borders Books & Music	Kukui Grove Center, Līhu'e	
Capricorn Fine Gems	Kauai Village, Kapa'a	245-6233
Collectibles & Fine Junque	9821 Kaumuali'i Hwy., Waimea	338-9855
Crazy Shirts	Anchor Cove Shopping Ctr.	245-7073
	5356 Kōloa Rd., Kōloa	742-7161
	Kauai Village, Kapa'a	823-6761
	Po'ipū Shopping Village	742-9000
Da Kine Floral Design	Po'ipū	742-6247
Flowers Forever	4139 Hardy, Līhu'e	245-4717
Gallery Hanalei	Hanalei	826-7006
Gem Dept. Store	Līhu'e Shopping Center	245-7391
Hanapepe Bookstore	3830 Hanapēpē Rd., Hanapēpē	335-5011
Hawaiian T-shirt & Hat Co.	Anahola	245-1790
Hilo Hattie's	3252 Kūhiō Hwy., Līhu'e	245-3404
Island Images	Coconut Marketplace, Kapa'a	822-3636
J C Penney	Kukui Grove Center, Līhu'e	245-5966
Jack Wada Electronics	2981 Umi, Līhu'e	245-3321
Kapaia Stitchery	Coconut Marketplace, Kapa'a	245-2281
Kauai Collectibles	1526 Kūhiō Hwy., Kapa'a	822-4281
Kauai Frame	3-4251 Kūhiō Hwy., Hanama'ulu	245-2199
Kauai Gold	Coconut Marketplace, Kapa'a	822-9361
Kauai Images	4-941 Kūhuō Hwy., Kapa'a	822-1950
Kilohana Galleries	3-2087 Kaumuali'i Hwy., Puhi	245-9352
Kong Lung Co.	Kīlauea	828-1822
James Hoyle Gallery	3900 Hanapēpē Rd., Hanapēpē	335-3582
Jim Saylor Jewelers	1318 Kūhiō Hwy., Kapa'a	822-3591
Kahn's Galleries	Coconut Marketplace, Kapa'a	822-4277
	Kilohana	246-4454
	Hanalei	826-6677
	Anchor Cove Shopping Ctr.	245-5397
Kashuba Fine Arts & Gold	Anchor Cove Shopping Ctr.	246-9088
Kauai Fruit & Flower Co.	3-4684 Kūhiō Hwy., Līhu'e	245-1814
Lee Sands	Hwy. 50 & Kōloa Rd., Lāwai	332-7404
Liberty House	Kukui Grove Center, Līhu'e	245-7751
	Coconut Marketplace, Kapa'a	822-3491
McInerny's	Hyatt Regency, Kōloa	742-2811
McInerny Waterware	1571 Po'ipū Rd., Po'ipū	742-2911
Overboard	Kiahuna Shopping Vill., Po'ipū	742-1299
Pictures Plus	Kukui Grove Center, Līhu'e	245-7111
Plantation Stitchery	Coconut Marketplace, Kapa'a	822-3570
Poi Pounder Shirts	Coconut Marketplace, Kapa'a	822-9080
Prestige Jewelers	Kukui Grove Center, Līhu'e	246-0888

Remember Kauai	Outrigger Kauai Beach	245-6650
	4-734 Kūhiō Hwy., Waipouli	822-0161
Robert's	3837 Hanapēpē Rd., Hanapēpē	335-5412
	2976 Kress St., Lihu'e	245-4653
Ruby Tuesday	Waipouli Town Center	822-0727
SanDudes Kauai	Princeville Center	826-7300
Sears	Kukui Grove Center, Lihu'e	245-3325
Shar's Scrimshaw	Kapa'a	822-9345
Shells International	Coconut Marketplace, Kapa'a	822-3781
Ship Store Galleries	4-484 Kūhiō Hwy., Kapa'a	822-4999
	Coconut Marketplace, Kapa'a	822-7758
	Po'ipū Shopping Village, Po'ipū	742-7123
Singer Hawaii	Kukui Grove Center, Lihu'e	245-5333
Swim Inn	5408 Kōloa Rd., Kōloa	742-1115
The Country Store	Kilohana	246-2778
The Goldsmith's Gallery	4-356 Kūhiō Hwy., Kapa'a	822-4653
Treasures of Kuan Yin	4504 Kukui, Kapa'a	822-1107
Tropical Shirts	Coconut Marketplace, Kapa'a	822-0203
	Kiahuna Shopping Vill., Po'ipū	742-6691
Tropical Tantrum	4-1296 Kūhiō Hwy., Kapa'a	822-7303
	Hanalei Center, Hanalei	826-6944
	4-941 Kūhiō Hwy., Kapa'a	822-1882
Vicky's Fabric Shop	4-1326 Kūhiō Hwy., Kapa'a	822-1746
Waldenbooks	Kukui Grove Center, Lihu'e	245-7162
	Coconut Marketplace, Kapa'a	822-9362
	Kauai Village, Kapa'a	822-7749
Wyland Galleries Hawaii	Kauai Village, Kapa'a	822-9855
	Anchor Cove Shopping Ctr.	246-0702
	Po'ipū Shopping Village, Po'ipū	742-6030
Ye Olde Ship Store	Coconut Marketplace, Kapa'a	822-1401

OTHER STORES & MARKETS

ABC Discount Stores	Anchor Cove Shopping Center	245-7071
	Kauai Village, Kapa'a	822-2115
	4-1259 Kūhiō Hwy., Kapa'a	823-0081
Ambrose's Kapuna Natural Foods	770 Kūhiō Hwy., Waipouli	822-7112
Big Save	Ele'ele	335-3127
	Waimea	338-1621
	Hanalei	826-6652
	Kapa'a	822-4971
	Kōloa	742-1614
	Lihu'e	245-6571
Discount Variety	3483 Weliweli Rd., Po'ipū	742-9393
Foodland Super Mkt.	Princeville	826-9880
	Waipouli Town Center	822-7271
General Nutrition Center	Kukui Grove Center, Lihu'e	245-6657

HPI Pharmacy	3420B Kūhiō Hwy., Līhu'e	245-2471
	Waimea	338-0600
Hale O Health	Rice Shopping Ctr., Līhu'e	245-9053
	Kīlauea	828-1021
Hanalei Health &		
Natural Foods	Ching Young Village, Hanalei	826-6990
Happy Kauaian	Coconut Marketplace, Kapa'a	822-5813
	Kauai Coconut Beach Resort	823-0761
	Lāwai	332-8536
	Wailua Marina, Wailua	822-5911
K-Mart	Kukui Grove Center, Līhu'e	245-7724
Long's Drug Store	Kukui Grove Center, Līhu'e	245-7771
Menehune Food Marts	Kīlauea	828-1771
	Kekaha Rd.	337-1335
	Lāwai	332-8641
	Kalāheo	332-7349
Menehune Pharmacy	1-9665 Kaumuali'i Hwy., Waimea	338-0200
North Shore Pharmacy	2460 Oka, Kīlauea	828-1844
Papaya's Garden Cafe		
& Market	Kauai Village, Kapa'a	823-0190
Pay Less Drug Stores	4100 Rice St., Līhu'e	245-6776
	Kauai Village, Kapa'a	822-4915
Pono Market	4-1300 Kūhiō Hwy., Kapa'a	822-4581
Safeway	Kauai Village, Kapa'a	822-2464
7-Eleven	3-3152 Kūhiō Hwy., Līhu'e	245-9422
	3-4340 Kūhiō Hwy., Hanamā'ulu	245-2110
Shoreview Pharmacy	4-1177 Kūhiō Hwy., Kapa'a	822-1447
Southshore Pharmacy	3176 Po'ipū Rd., Kōloa	822-1447
Star Markets	Kukui Grove Center, Līhu'e	245-7777
Village Variety	Ching Young Village, Hanalei	826-6077
Wainiha General Store	Wainiha	926-6251
Waipouli Variety	4-901 Kūhiō Hwy., Waipouli	822-1014
Westside Pharmacy	1-3845 Kaumuali'i Hwy., Hanapēpē	335-5342
Woolworth	Kukui Grove Center, Līh'ue	245-7702

SHOPPING CENTERS

Anchor Cove Center	3501 Rice St., Nāwiliwili	246-0634
Ching Young Village	5-5190 Kūhiō Hwy., Hanalei	826-7222
Coconut Marketplace	484 Kūhiō Hwy., Kapa'a	822-3641
Hanalei Center	Kūhiō Hwy., Hanalei	826-7677
Kauai Village	Kūhiō Hwy., Kapa'a	822-4904
Kilohana	3-2087 Kaumuali'i Hwy., Puhi	254-5608
Kong Lung Center	Lighthouse Rd., Kīlauea	828-6616
Kukui Grove Center	Kaumualii Hwy., Līhu'e	245-7784
Pacific Ocean Plaza	Nāwiliwili Harbor	245-5919
Poipu Shopping Village	Po'ipū	246-0634
Princeville Center	Princeville	826-3040
Rice Shopping Center	4303 Rice St., Līhu'e	245-2033
Waipouli Town Center	Waipouli (Oahu) -	524-2023

PLACES OF INTEREST

Fern Grotto	(Smith's Motor Boat Service)	822-5213
	(Wai'ale'ale Boat Tours)	822-4908
Hawaiian Art Museum	2488 Kolo Rd., Kīlauea	245-6931
Kamokila Hawaiian Village	6060 Kuamo'o Rd., Kapa'a	822-1192
Kauai Museum	4428 Rice St., Līhu'e	245-6931
Kīlauea Lighthouse	Kīlauea, end of Lighthouse Rd.	
Kilohana	3-2087 Kaumuali'i Hwy., Līhu'e	245-5608
Kōke'e Natural History Museum	Kōke'e Rd. (16 mi. marker), Kōke'e	335-9975
Kukui o Lono	Pāpālima Rd., Kalāheo	
Lutheran Church (Built in 1883)	4602 Ho'omana Rd., Līhu'e	245-2145
Menehune Gardens	Nāwiliwili	245-2660
National Tropical Botanical Garden	Hailima Road, Kalāheo	332-7361
Old Kōloa Town	Kōloa Rd.	
'Olu Pua Botanical Gardens	Kalāheo	332-8182
Salt Ponds	Hanapēpē	
Smith's Tropical Paradise	Marina State Park, Wailua	822-4654
Waioli Mission House Museum	Kūhiō Hwy., Hanalei	245-3202

HAWAIIAN WORD LIST

These words are likely to be seen or heard by anyone visiting these islands. Some may be seen without the markings that alter pronunciation (and meaning), as explained in the INTRODUCTION. In the pronunciation guides given here, typical English syllables which most closely approximate the Hawaiian vowel sounds are used; a precise rendition would require long and complex explanations. The 'okina (glottal stop) has been retained to show where adjacent vowels should not slide from one to the other. The kahakō (macron) shows where they are especially joined, almost as English diphthongs; syllables with elongated vowels are written twice and linked with the same mark. Stress is indicated by capitalization.

a'ā (AH-'AH) a rough, crumbly type of lava
aikāne (aye-KAH-neh) friend
akamai (ah-kah-my-ee) smart, wise, on the ball
ali'i (ah-LEE-'ee) chief, nobility
aloha a nui loa (ah-LO-ha ah NOO-ee LO-ah) much love
auē, auwē (ah-oo-EH-EH) alas!, oh dear!, too bad!, goodness!
'awa (AH-vah) traditional Polynesian drink wrung from the roots of the pepper plant
hana hou (hah-nah HO-oo) encore, do it again

hanohano (hah-no-HAH-no) distinguished, magnificent
haole (HAH-oh-leh) originally foreigner; now Caucasian
hapa (HAH-pa) half, part
hapa-haole (HAH-pa HAH-oh-leh) half Caucasian
Hauʻoli Makahiki Hou (ha-oo-ʻoh-lee mah-ka-hee-kee ho-oo) Hawaiian
  translation of Happy New Year (now used, but not traditional greeting)
haupia (ha-oo-PEE-ah) coconut pudding
heiau (HEH-ee-ah-oo) ancient Hawaiian place of worship
hele (HEH-leh) go, walk around
holoholo (ho-lo-HO-lo) to visit about, make the rounds
holokū (ho-LO-koo) a fitted, ankle-length dress, sometimes with train
hoʻolauleʻa (ho-ʻoh-lah-oo-LAY-ah) celebration
hui (HOO-ee) club, association
hukilau (HOO-kee-lah-oo) community net-fishing party
hula (HOO-lah) Hawaiian dance
huli (HOO-lee) turn over, turn around
humuhumunukunukuāpuaʻa (hoo-moo-hoo-moo-noo-koo-noo-koo-ah-poo-
  AH-ʻah) Hawaiʻi's state fish; a small triggerfish famous for its long name
iki (EE-kee) little (size)
imu (EE-moo) ground oven
imua (ee-MOO-ah) forward, onward
kāhili (kah-ah-HEE-lee) a royal feathered standard
kahuna (kah-HOO-nah) priest, expert
kai (KY-ee) sea, sea water
kālā (KAH-lah) money (literally dollar)
kamaʻāina (kah-mah-AYE-nah) native born, longtime Hawaiʻi resident, old
  established family
kanaka (ka-NAH-kah) originally 'man' or person; now a native Hawaiian
kāne (KAH-neh) boy, man, husband
kapa (KAH-pah) tapa cloth (made from mulberry bark)
kapakahi (kah-pah-KAH-hee) crooked, lopsided
kapu (KAH-poo) forbidden, sacred, taboo, keep out
kaukau (KAH-oo-kah-oo) food
keiki (KAY-kee) child
kiawe (kee-AH-vay) mesquite tree
kōkua (ko-KOO-ah) help, assistance, aid
kona (KO-nah) winds 'that blow against the trades', lee side of an island
kukui (koo-KOO-ee) candlenut tree
kumu (KOO-moo) teacher
lānai (lah-NY-ee) porch, terrace, veranda
lani (LAH-nee) heaven, heavenly, sky
lauhala (lah-oo-HAH-lah) leaf of the pandanus tree (for weaving)
laulau (LAH-oo-lah-oo) bundled food in ti leaves
lei (LAY-ee) garland of flowers, shells or feathers, wreath
lilikoʻi (lee-lee-KOH-ee) passion fruit
loa (LO-ah) long
lomi (LO-mee) rub, press, massage, type of raw salmon (usually lomilomi)
lua (LOO-ah) toilet, restroom
lūʻau (LOO-ʻah-oo) feast, party, taro leaf

mahalo (mah-HAH-loh) thank you
mahimahi (mah-hee-MAH-hee) dorado or dolphin fish
māhū (MAH-hoo) gay, homosexual
makai (mah-KY-ee) toward the sea
make (MAH-keh) dead
makule (mah-KOO-leh) elderly, old (of people)
malihini (mah-lee-HEE-nee) newcomer, visitor
malo (MAH-lo) man's loincloth
mauka (MAH-oo-ka) toward the mountains, inland
mauna (MAH-oo-nah) mountain
Mele Kalikimaka (meh-leh kah-lee-kee-MAH-ka) Merry Christmas
Menehune (meh-neh-HOO-neh) legendary race of dwarfs
moemoe (mo-eh-MO-eh) sleep
mu'umu'u (moo-'oo-moo-'oo) long or short loose-fitting dress
nui (NOO-ee) big
'ohana (oh-HAH-nah) family, extended family
'ōkole (oh-oh-KO-lay) buttocks, bottom, rear
'ōkole maluna (oh-oh-ko-lay-mah-LOO-nah) Hawaiian translation
    of 'bottoms up' (a bit crude)
'ono (OH-no) delicious
'ōpu (OH-OH-POO-OO) abdomen, stomach
pakalōlō (pah-kah-LO-lo) marijuana
Pākē (PAH-keh) Chinese
pali (PAH-lee) cliff, precipice; the Pali= Nu'uanu Pali (O'ahu)
paniolo (pah-nee-OH-lo) cowboy
pau (PA-oo) finished, done
pau hana (pa-oo HAH-nah) finish work
pāhoehoe (pah-ho-eh-HO-eh) type of lava with smooth or ropy surface
pīkake (pee-KAH-keh) jasmine flower, named after 'peacock'
poi (POY) pasty starch made from pounded taro
puka (POO-kah) hole, door
pūpū (POO-poo) hors d'oeuvres (literally 'shells')
tūtū (TOO-TOO) grandmother, affectionate term for old people--relatives or
    friends--of grandparents' generation (according to the rules of language set
    down by the missionaries, there is no 't' in the Hawaiian language, but
    hardly anyone ever says kūkū)
'uku (OO-koo) fleas, head lice
'ukulele (oo-koo-LAY-leh) small, stringed instrument from Portugal
wahine (va-HEE-neh, wah-HEE-neh) girl, woman, wife
wikiwiki (wee-kee-WEE-kee) fast, in a hurry, quickly

PIDGIN ENGLISH WORDS

The pronunciation of pidgin is self-evident, and its spelling is phonic rather than fixed. In most cases, the derivation is also obvious. The lilt that is peculiar to this local lingo cannot be adequately described; it must be heard. This list is given as a guide to listening only. Trying to speak pidgin involves the risk of inadvertently saying something offensive or insulting. Everyone who speaks pidgin also understands correctly spoken English.

an den? So? What next? What else? (and then)
any kine anything (any kind)
ass right you are correct (that's right)
bambucha big
bambula big
blalah heavy-set, Hawaiian man, may be looking for a fight
bradah friend (brother)
brah short for bradah
buggah guy, friend, pest
bumbye after a while (by and by)
bummahs too bad, disappointed expression (bummer)
cockaroach rip off, steal, confiscate
cool head main ting keep calm, relax
da the
da kine anything being discussed, used as either noun or verb when the speaker can't think of the right word
dat that
dem them, guys, folks
eh? you know, do you understand?; also used at the beginning of a statement
garans guaranteed, for sure
geevum go for it! (give them)
grind eat
grinds food
had it destroyed, wrecked
haaah? what? I didn't hear you
haolefied like a haole
hele on go, leave, 'with it', 'hip'
high mucka mucka arrogant, conceited, elite
ho! exclamation used before a strong statement
how you figga? how do you figure that, makes no sense
howzit hi, hello, how are you doing, what's happening (how is it)
junk lousy, terrible
kay den okay then, fine
li'dat like that, shortcut for lengthy explanation
li'dis like this
humbug trouble, bother
make 'A' make a fool of yourself (make ass)
make house make yourself at home, act like you own the place
mama-san local Japanese equivalent of 'mom' at 'mom and 'pop' stores

Maui wowie potent marijuana from Maui
minors no big thing, minor
mo' more
mo' bettah better, good stuff
moke heavy-set Hawaiian male, often looking for a fight
nah just kidding (often **nah, nah, nah**)
no can cannot, I can't do it
o' wot? (added on to most questions, usually when the speaker is fed up -- or what?)
poi dog mut, person made up of many ethnic mixtures
shahkbait white-skinned, pale (shark bait)
shaka all right, great, well done, perfect, okay, right on
sleepahs flip-flops, thongs (slippers)
stink eye dirty look, evil eye
talk story rap, shoot the breeze, gossip
tanks, eh? thank you
tita heavy-set Hawaiian woman, may be looking for a fight (sister)
try used at beginning of a command
we go let's leave
yeah? added on to the end of sentences
yeah yeah yeah yeah yes, all right, shut up

RECOMMENDED READING

There are countless books detailing the many aspects of Hawaiian history and culture, both ancient and modern. It has been impossible to detail these fascinating areas in a guidebook small enough to be handy. We recommend the following:

Atlas of Hawaii, by the Dept. of Geography, University of Hawai'i; University of Hawai'i Press, 1983. This book provides text on Hawai'i's natural environment, culture and economy along with maps.

The Beaches of Kaua'i County, by John R. K. Clark, University of Hawai'i Press. A complete guide to all the beaches of Kaua'i County, with maps, photographs, descriptions of facilities, emergency aid, suitability for various water activities, and legends and lore associated with each area.

Bird Life in Hawaii, by Andrew J. Berger, Island Heritage, 1987. The story of the bird life in Hawai'i, including exotic birds and species which have become rare and endangered, each illustrated in full color accompanied by text written by the world's leading authority on Hawaiian birds.

Discovery, The Hawaiian Odyssey, Bishop Museum Press, 1993. This exquisitely designed coffee table book chronicles the dramatic saga of Polynesian exploration, celebrating the genius of ancient navigators and the triumph of Hawaiian civilization.

Entertaining Island Style, by Lavonne Tollerud and Barbara Gray, Island Heritage, 1987. Menu planning is made simple in this colorful book.

From *lu'au* and beach parties to elegant Hawaiian suppers, there are many creative ideas for entertaining.

Favorite Recipes from Hawaii, by Lavonne Tollerud and Barbara Gray, Island Heritage, 1987. A collection of Hawai'i's most popular recipes. It includes Hawaiian cocktails, hors d'oeuvres, soups, salads, breads, main dishes, condiments, rice and noodles, vegetables and desserts.

Flowers of Hawaii, photography by Allan Seiden and Loye Gutherie, Island Heritage, 1987. A beautifully photographed guide to Hawai'i's colorful flowers, such as hibiscus, orchids and lilies, and their origins.

A Guide to Hawaiian Marine Life, by Les Matsuura, Island Heritage, 1987. Written by a marine educator at the Waikīkī Aquarium, this guide highlights the marine life in Hawai'i through description and color photographs.

Hawai'i, by Moana Tregaskis, Compass American Guides, 1992. Explore Hawai'i with *New York Times* travel writer Moana Tregaskis, who blends the insights of a native with the perspective of a sophisticated international traveler. Detailed facts of every aspect of island culture, history and places of interest, complete with superb color photographs.

Hawaii, by James Michener, Random, 1959. A novel about Hawai'i from its geological birth to the present, by this famous author. Mixing historical facts with fictions, this book makes a very engaging and interesting reading.

Hawaii: A History, by Ralph S. Kuykendall, Prentice, 1961. A good and read-able overall history of Hawai'i from the first Polynesian voyages to statehood.

Hawaii: The Aloha State, by Allan Seiden, Island Heritage, 1987. Visit exciting Waikīkī, colorful Lahaina, majestic Waimea Canyon, historic Kona--all the Hawaiian Islands are brought to life in this beautifully photographed book.

Hawaii Below: Favorites, Tips and Secrets of the Diving Pros, written and photographed by Rod Canham. Touted by Hawai'i's diving community as the ultimate resource for diving Hawai'i's waters, this island-by-island guide is a wealth of inside information drawn from the author's own experiences and those of numerous diving pros.

Hawaiian Dictionary, by Mary Kawena Pukui and Samuel H. Elbert, University of Hawai'i Press, 1986. Hawaiian-English, English-Hawaiian dictionary, regarded as the definitive reference for Hawaiian vocabulary. It contains folklore, poetry and ethnology compiled by the leading authorities of Hawaiian and Polynesian languages.

Hawaii's Humpback Whales: A Complete Whalewatchers Guide, by Gregory D. Kaufman and Paul H. Forestall, Pacific Whale Foundation. Everything you ever wanted to know about humpback whales is provided in this fascinating book.

Hiking Kauai, by Robert Smith, Wilderness Press, 1983. This guidebook lists hiking trails on Kaua'i, all personally trod by the author, with descriptions of the route, highlights, rating of difficulty, driving instructions, distance and average hiking time.

Historic Kōloa: A Guide, by Friends of the Kōloa Community, Friends of the Kōloa Community-School Library, 1985. Compiled by a group of volunteers who interviewed old-timers, and combed archival and library sources for interesting old photographs and details of community history, this book presents a fascinating glimpse of the history of this charming Kaua'i sugar town.

The Illustrated Atlas of Hawaii, by Gavan Daws, O. A. Bushnell & Andrew Berger, Island Heritage, 1987. Illustrations of the Hawaiian island chain, native plants, birds and fish by Joseph Feher with a concise history.

The Journal of Prince Alexander Liholiho, Jacob Adler, ed., University of Hawai'i Press, 1967. Young Alexander Liholiho and his brother Lot visited the United States, England and France on a diplomatic mission. This diary records the impressions of the future king.

Kaaawa: A Novel about Hawaii in the 1850s, by Oswald Bushnell, University of Hawai'i Press, 1972. Historical novel set on O'ahu about the missionary period.

Ka'ahumanu: Molder of Change, by Jane Silverman, Friends of the Judiciary History Center of Hawaii, 1987. A biography of the most powerful woman in Hawaiian history and the vast changes she wrought in the social and political life of the kingdom she ruled.

Kahuna La'au Lapa'au (The Practice of Hawaiian Herbal Medicine), by June Gutmanis, Island Heritage, 1987. Authoritative and definitive work on Hawaiian herbs and the secrets of Hawaiian herbal medicine, with colorful illustrations.

Kalakaua: Hawaii's Last King, by Kristin Zambucka, Mana Publishing Co. and Marvin/Richard Enterprises, Inc., 1983. This pictorial biography with more than 180 old photographs recounts the colorful reign of Hawai'i's last king.

Kauai, by Allan Seiden, Island Heritage, 1986. Seiden's photographs of beaches and sight-seeing spots come alive in this brief overview of the island.

Kauai: A Many Splendored Island, by Ronn Ronck, Mutual Publishing, 1985. This large format book presents splendid photographs by Douglas Peebles showing the many faces of Kaua'i. The text provides details and descriptions of the scenes, and provides glimpses of island history.

The Kauai Album, by Carol Wilcox, Kauai Historical Society, 1981. Enriched with many old photographs, this survey tells a lot about the island's European history, tracing the growth from villages of seven of Kaua'i's current towns, and presenting details of more than a hundred of Kaua'i's historically significant buildings.

Kauai: The Garden Isle, by Allan Seiden, Island Heritage, 1986. This colorful pictorial work explores the magic and beauty of the island including how it was formed, its history, and breathtaking views of different areas.

Na Pule Kahiko: Ancient Hawaiian Prayers, by June Gutmanis, Editions Limited, 1983. This collection of traditional Hawaiian prayers, in both Hawaiian and English, is annotated with fascinating detail about the contexts in which these prayers, and prayers in general, were used in the lives of ancient Hawaiians.

Niihau Shell Leis, by Linda Paik Moriarty, University of Hawai'i Press, 1986. An expert documentation of the traditions of this unique art, richly illustrated with color photographs of the many varieties of this rare and precious, gem-quality shell. Based on personal interviews with Ni'ihau women who are actively engaged in this ancient craft.

An Ocean Mind, by Will Kyselka, University of Hawai'i Press, 1987. The extraordinary story of a 6000-mile trip from Hawai'i to Tahiti and back, the 1980 voyage of the Hokule'a, without the use of modern navigational aid. Navigator Nainoa Thompson, of Hawaiian descent, studied the stars, winds and currents to explore his Polynesian past.

Place Names of Hawaii, by Mary Kawena Pukui, Samuel H. Elbert & Esther T. Mookini, University of Hawai'i Press, 1974. Place names listed with pronunciation and translation where known. Includes names of valleys, streams, mountains, land sections, surfing areas, towns, villages and Honolulu streets and buildings.

Princess Kaiulani: The Last Hope of Hawai'i's Monarchy, by Kristin Zambucka, Mana Publishing Co., 1982. Pictorial biography of Hawai'i's beautiful and tragic princess. Niece of Queen Lili'uokalani, Hawai'i's last reigning monarch, Princess Ka'iulani was next in the line of succession to the throne.

Pua Nani, by Jeri Bostwick, photographs by Douglas Peebles, Mutual Publishing, 1987. Stunning color photography of the myriad blossoms--both native and introduced--that festoon these islands with their glorious hues and intricate structures.

Reflections of Kauai, by Penny Pence Smith, Island Heritage Publishing, 1989. More than 200 splendid color photographs of Kauai lifestyle and landscapes, accompanied by an essay on the history, culture and character of the Garden Isle.

The Return of Lono, by Oswald Bushnell, University of Hawai'i Press, 1971. A fictional reconstruction of the discovery of the Hawaiian Islands by Captain Cook.

Shoal of Time, by Gavan Daws, University of Hawai'i Press, 1974. An excellent and authoritative history of Hawai'i from earliest times to statehood in 1959.

Tropical Drinks and Pupus from Hawaii, by Lavonne Tollerud and Barbara Gray, Island Heritage, 1987. Delicious island cocktails and fruit drinks are complemented with a wide range of Hawaiian-style hors d'oeuvres.

The Wilcox Quilts in Hawaii, by Robert J. Schleck, Grove Farm Homestead & Waioli Mission House, 1987. This lovely book not only presents beautiful color photographs of the entire collection of quilts held by Grove Farm Homestead, but gives an interesting historic account as well.

INDEX

PHOTOGRAPHERS

iii	Scott Rutherford	Wailua Falls
1	Monte Costa	Leave Textures
3	Scott Rutherford	Hanalei Bay/Bali Hai
5	Scott Rutherford	Taro Fields in Hanalei
6	Veronica Carmona	Secret Beach
7	Scott Rutherford	Deserted Beaches
9	Peter French	Kilauea Wildlife Santuary
10	David Cornwell	Etched Nā Pali Coast
11	Scott Rutherford	Waimea Canyon
12	Scott Rutherford	Twilight/Waimea
14	Bob Abraham	Hawaiian State Flag
15	David Cornwell	Glory bush/vriesea flowers
16	Ann Cecil	Sunset/Nā Pali Coast
17	David Cornwell	Aeriel view of upcountry
18	Scott Rutherford	Po'ipū Beach, sunset
19	Ann Cecil	Menehune Fishponds
21	Scott Rutherford	Taro Farmer harvesting
23	Scott Rutherford	Afternoon at Brennecke's Beach
25	Bob Abraham	Aerial view of Nā Pali Coast
27	Bob Abraham	Zodiac braves rough waters
29	Peter French	Wailua River
31	David Cornwell	Sailboat
33	Scott Rutherford	Beachcombers
34	David Cornwell	Nā Pali Coast
35	Scott Rutherford	Strong currents at Hanalei Bay
36	Scott Rutherford	Kiki a Ola, the Menehune Ditch
37	Scott Rutherford	Waimea Canyon
39	Scott Rutherford	Princeville Aeriel
40	David Cornwell	Fern Grotto
41	Scott Rutherford	Waimea Canyon
43	Scott Rutherford	Russian Fort Elizabeth
46	Scott Rutherford	Offerings at Hauola Pu'uhonua
48	Scott Rutherford	Rainbow at Waimea
49	David Cornwell	Afternoon at Nā Pali Coast
50	David Cornwell	Kalalau Valley
51	Scott Rutherford	Polihale Beach
52	Scott Rutherford	Hā'ena Point
56	Scott Rutherford	Building Sand Castles
59	Scott Rutherford	Hanalei
63	Scott Rutherford	Sunset/Kaua'i's South Shore
65	Bob Abraham	Fishing Boat in Sunset
67	Bob Abraham	Scuba Diver
68	Scott Rutherford	Snorkeling Kids
71	Scott Rutherford	Surfing Family
73	Scott Rutherford	Kayaking
75	David Cornwell	Horseback Riding/Princeville
78	Scott Rutherford	Rocky Shores/Polihale Beach
81	Ruth Gurnani-Smith	Hanakāpī'ai Beach/Kalalau Trail
83	Bob Abraham	Hawaiian Maiden
86	Peter French	Keiki Hula
88	Bob Abraham	Entertainers at Fern Grotto
93	Joe Carini	Leis of Aloha
100	Mark Stephenson	Ni'ihau Shell Lei
103	Hyatt Regency Kauai	Elegant Grass Shack Dining
104	Hyatt Regency Kauai	Dining with Waterfall
114	Island Heritage Photo	Food display at 'Ōpaeka'a Falls
123	Hyatt Regency Kauai	Lagoon front
124	Hyatt Regency Kauai	Lounge Area
128	Scott Rutherford	Princeville aerial
135	Scott Rutherford	Sunset walk/Po'ipū beach
144	Peter French	Haena Beach
149	Scott Rutherford	Clouds
151	Scott Rutherford	Newly Wed Couple
152	Scott Rutherford	Kid with boogie board
155	Scott Rutherford	Cane Fields

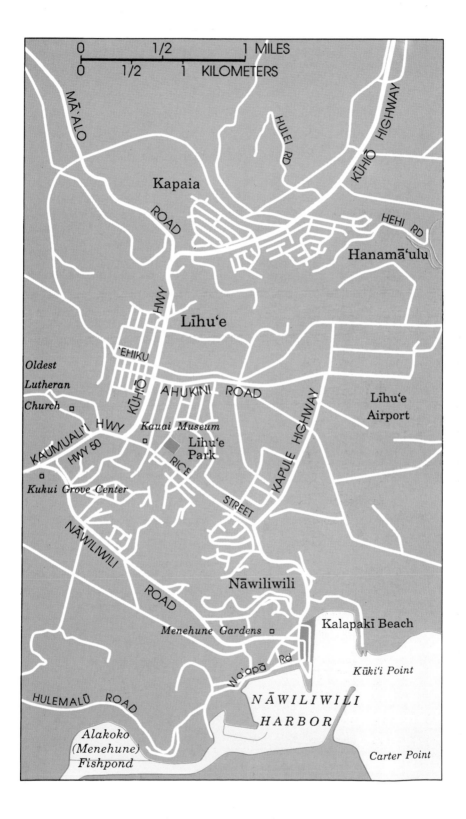

0   1/2   1 MILES
0   1/2   1 KILOMETERS

MĀʻALO

Kapaia

ROAD

HUIEI RD

KŪHIŌ HIGHWAY

HEHI RD

Hanamāʻulu

HWY

Līhuʻe

ʻEHIKU

KŪHIŌ

AHUKINI ROAD

Oldest
Lutheran
Church □

KAUMUALIʻI HWY

HWY 50

Kauai Museum □

Līhuʻe
Park

RICE

KAPULE HIGHWAY

Līhuʻe
Airport

□

Kukui Grove Center

NĀWILIWILI

ROAD

STREET

Nāwiliwili

Menehune Gardens □

Kalapakī Beach

Kūkiʻi Point

Waʻapā Rd

NĀWILIWILI
HARBOR

HULEMALŪ ROAD

Alakoko
(Menehune)
Fishpond

Carter Point

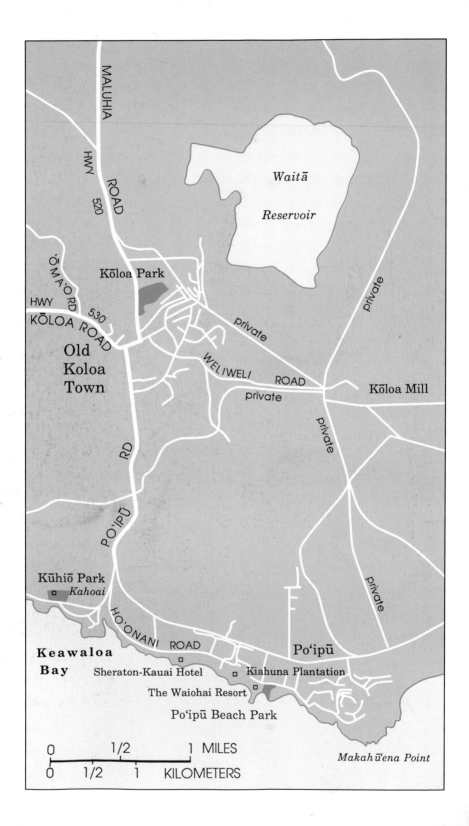

MALUHIA

HWY
520

ROAD

'ŌMA'O RD

HWY
530

KŌLOA ROAD

Kōloa Park

Old
Koloa
Town

Waitā

Reservoir

private

private

WELIWELI

ROAD

private

Kōloa Mill

private

PO'IPŪ

RD

Kūhiō Park

Kahoai

private

HO'ONANI

ROAD

Keawaloa
Bay

Sheraton-Kauai Hotel

The Waiohai Resort

Po'ipū Beach Park

Kiahuna Plantation

Po'ipū

Makahū'ena Point

0   1/2   1 MILES
0   1/2   1   KILOMETERS